TYRIK COGDELL

I0161017

WAKE UP
BLACK PEOPLE
OR DIE

INTRODUCTION

Black power to all my people! My name is Tyrik Cogdell. I'm a thirdly seven year old foundational black American man who grew up in the late eighties in the south Bronx of new York city. I'm a husband and a father to three beautiful children. I'm making this book to open up black people eyes to white supremacy, in order to defend ourselves from their evil, corrupted ways. Unfortunately I don't have the commanding presence, skills or voice to lead our people like many past great black leaders like Malcom X, Martin Luther King Jr, Huey Newton, Bobby Seale, Eldridge & Kathleen Cleaver along with Fred Hampton and so many more black revolution leaders. However, I might not be able to lead our people towards liberation, But god has bless me with the ability to write and the will to publish my thoughts on paper, So that's the part I will play in this revolution. If I'm able to open just one black man or woman eyes open to the evil that is white supremacy, Then I know had contribute to the cause of liberating our people towards real freedom.

Chapter One

WHITE SUPREMACY

White Supremacy is a term meaning that white people are the superior race on the planted, Especially over the black race. Now I want to explain that the whole world is ruled by white supremacy ideology. White supremacy is not just a USA thing it is a global empire. In order to be an white supremist you don't have to be a true Caucasian (white) to practice white supremacy. You can be a white supremist and be black, you see them all the time on television, your neighborhoods and in work places. The coons and coonets, The sell outs who bash and degrade our people everyday, Especially the foundational black Americans. We are killed and hunted down in the streets like rapid animals, we are given no justice but we are always asked to forgive and forget and if we don't we are demonized. We have no power, No structure, Even Africa is run by white supremist and yes that includes the chinses as well. But no matter how overwhelming white supremacy may seem we can overcome it, It will be hell to endure, But we been enduring hell for over four hundred years underneath the white man. They going to treat us like dirt anyway so let us give them hell in the process. Everything been taken from us and yet we always found a way to rise, while the white supremist are giving every advantage and yet they still fear us, Because they know if only an quarter of us get on code and unite their world will crash and burn. Another way white supremacy uses their power to oppressed our people is through the education system. Urban schools that mostly have a black populace are over crowed with less funding for books, computers and other school supplies. Everything I've learned about my people history I learned on my own, outside of the public school system but more importantly the actual lies that are told to our youth about the history of this country is sickening. When I was in school one of the many lies that the white supremacy education system taught us was that Christopher Columbus discovered the United States of America. How he was a true hero who discovered the new world. Christopher Columbus never set sails on what we now called the United States of America. The very fact that you could say with a straight face that anyone could discovered a land already full of people and name it whatever they like, Is a evil act of terrorism in my eyes. White supremacy is a invading force that took native Americans and aboriginals black peoples land by force and then made a holiday about it, calling it Thanksgiving. Christopher Columbus ship landed on a place named Hispaniola in 1492 which is now called Haiti and the Dominican Republic. Christopher Columbus took advantage of the natives (black people) of the land and brutally killed them, Rape them and made them slaves as he became ruler over their land. Christopher Columbus also took over the Bahama and the coast of central and south America enslaving the people there. Christopher Columbus returned to Spain with over five hundred enslaved blacks/ native people who lived on those lands. Christopher Columbus was not a hero but a white supremist who murdered, enslaved, Even rape and sold nine and ten year old little girls. Which made him a rapist and pedophilia. Christopher Columbus once wrote. "A hundred castellanos are as easily obtained for a woman as for a farm, And it is very general and there are plenty of dealers who go about looking for girls, Those from nine to ten are now in demand." This pedophilia wrote.

Christopher Columbus close friend Michele Decuneo wrote his first encounter with an native black girl that Columbus gave to him as a gift. "While I was in the boat I captured a very beautiful Carib woman, whom the lord admiral gave to me. And with whom, having taken her in to my cabin, She being naked according to their custom, I conceived desire to take pleasure. I wanted to put my desire in to execution but she did not want it and treated me with her finger nails in such a manner that I wished I had never begun. But seeing that I took a rope and trashed her well, for which she raised such unheard of screams that you would not have believed your ears. Finally we came to an agreement in such manner that I can tell you that she seemed to have been brought up in a school of Harlots." This rapist gloated. The 3rd president of the united states who help create the Declaration of Independence was also a slave owner who owned over 200 enslaved black men, women and children. But worst just like a lot of the white supremist he was an pedophile rapist. Thomas Jefferson own an enslaved girl named Sally Hemings who was the half sister of his late wife Martha Wayles Skelton Jefferson, Because they shared the same father named John Wayles. Just like John Wayles would rape Sally mother Betty Hemings. Thomas Jefferson was constantly rapping the 14 year old Sally while they stayed in Paris, Impregnating her, Sally child died when they return back to America. Jefferson continues to rape Sally as she gave birth to six of his offspring's in Monticello New York. The Greeks, the Romans, Europe and America, you can see that pedophile is very important to white supremacy culture. Christopher Columbus unofficially started the Atlantic slave trade before the official date of Spain/ portaged was enslaving black Brazilians across the Atlantic in 1526. Another example of the corruption of our school system for black people are in many cities of the united states that have a heavy populace of white people, the schools will make rules to discouraged young black people mainly girls from embracing their natural hair styles in school by banding Afros, Braids, Dreadlocks and extensions in schools. Not allowing a young black woman name Amari Williams to attend her prom for wearing an African dress to prom or kicking out a black young man named Nyree Holmes from his graduation for wearing a traditional African kente cloth around his shoulders or how a group of African American students were forcefully yank off stage for celebration their collage graduation. So on and so on these stories continues here in the land of the free. You also must learn that under this white supremacy system, that we all live under, we do not have the same rights as white people. I'll repeat we do not have the same rights as white people. We live in a full police state in the United States of America, Especially in urban areas where there are a large number of foundational black American people. Example of our rights not being the same despite the letter of the law. One of the most popular things that white people are doing now is weaponizing 9-1-1 calls against black people. Everyday you turn around there is a white woman calling the police on us for just living life. Little girl selling water in new York, Call the police. Black people at a BBQ, Call police. Siting down in Starbucks, Call the police, using the bathroom in Starbucks, Call the police. Entering your apartment complex, sleeping in your collage dorm, reading in your collage dorm, moving in to a nice house, the white supremist calls 9-1-1. There are plenty more examples but you get the point. There is an law about 9-1-1 abuse and white people are getting a past for it. this weaponize use of 9-1-1 on black people for non emergency calls are being use all around the united states of America. There was a video where a white officer defended a white woman by saying that "she was in her right to call 9-1-1 as many times as she wants." Now flip it around where black people calling the police for false or stupid reasons. A black man calls 9-1-1 about a movie he didn't like and receives an fine, A black woman calls the cops on her man because she thinks he's cheating a police officer threating to write her a summons. When we call 9-1-1 about bull crap we get fined or arrested, white people call the cops on us nothing happens to them. That is white privilege at it's finest. My black people by the way never, ever call the cops on each other unless it's a possible life or death situation because if it's not an emergency you are putting that person and even possibly your own life in danger. Another of this double standard society against black people which is very disturbing to me is Florida's stand your ground law. Stand your ground is a white supremist wet dream. There is more than a 90% chance if a white man shoots and kills a black person because he feels threating, the white supremist knows the law won't convict them of a crime just like they didn't convict George Zimmerman who stalk, shot and murdered Trayvon Martin. Then there's a black woman named Marissa Alexander who was convicted for twenty years and spent six years in jail for shooting a warning shot at her abusive husband that was attacking her. But if we don't be silent and take the fight to these people we can force a change, Because of our outrage and public attention we made about Trayvon Martin, Marissa case got notice and helped her get free while causing two white supremist to pay for the killing of Jordan Davis for playing loud music in his car, with a conviction of life in jail. Now we must get this stand your ground law abolish all together for there won't be no more Trayvon Martins, Jordan Davis, Markeis Mcglockton and many more who was murdered because an white supremist felt protected by this unjust law. Everyday they work on new ways to oppress us, so every day we must continues to fight and overcome their murdering, oppressive racist ways. They had enslaved us, rape us, stripe us of our culture and history, they beat and kill us and yet here we are, still rising from the pits of hell they created for us and they fear us for it.

Chapter Two

SLAVERY

What if I told you that slavery never ended in 1865. that it's very much still alive till this very day in America. You would think I'm crazy but it's true, America never ended slavery. All you have to do is look at the united states 13th amendment in the constitution of the bill of rights. The 13th amendment states "Neither slavery nor involuntary servitude, Except as punishment for crime where of the party shall have been duly convicted, shall exist within the united states, or any place subject to their jurisdiction." Meaning you are only free until you get convicted of a crime, which you will once again become a slave under the united states of America until your time is served. Once you are a prisoner/ slave under federal prison and state prisons unlike most state jails which only extra privilege can be taking away like TV, money any yard time. prisons if you refuse to work, you will be put in the hole/ Segregation. No visitors in many prisons, No privileges. Just three meals in a lonely cell. In some cases they will add to your sentence if you continues not to work. There has been plenty of reports in southern states like Arizona and Texas are known to assault their prisoners/ slaves by beating them or spraying them down with pepper spray until they give in. It's very effective. Prisoners/ Slaves are now rented to private corporations to do labor, field work, factory work, All for ten cent a hour or an dollar a day. You also lose many rights as an u.s civilian by being a convicted felon. You can't vote, your right to bare arms are gone, you can't join the military, Good luck getting any business loans(it's hard as hell to get one with a clean record as a black man/woman) Many apartment complexes don't accept felons as well. And of course no decent job really hire felons, Especially black ones. Which leads you a very good chance of becoming a slave again for the united states of America. If you thinking just stay out of trouble and don't be another thug or hood rat and you won't be arrested, you won't become another slave in prison, if you believe that, then you are delusional black people. You must have seen it by now the double standards of the law for black & white people. it is a proven fact that white men are responsible for more violent crimes such as murders and rape in this country then black people, but yet the black man is convicted with crimes more often and sentence with harsher jail time for the same and lesser crimes then his white counterpart. Remember when the Clintons called the black youth super predators. When they we're locking up our youth, the crack users and dealers with harsh time on the ' War on Drugs' while now that white people are addicted to meth and opioids it's called mental health problems. How many times have you heard a black man was release from prison after years of slavery because a white woman false accused them of rape. they were convicted not because of evidence but because they couldn't afford a decent lawyer or because the jury was completely white. Famous black athletes can barely escape the lies of the white woman who cries rape, like Kobe Bryant or Dereck rose of the NBA . Whereas a white man can rape a woman of any color even white, If he's young or have a decent government job can get of with probation or a year or two on house arrest. As the judge states he don't want to ruin the young white man's life because of a terrible mistake, Now if a black man is even accused of rape, even being young as fifteen years of age can be charged to the full extent of the law. Young black boys always been premier to the slave master. Don't forget the race solider/ slave patrol cops who plant drugs on innocent black men, Forcing them to plead to lesser jail sentencing because they scare of facing a loner time in prison if convicted in a court trail, knowing that they can't afford a decent lawyer. Most black people are in prison for nonviolent crimes, which many are also falsely convicted of, whereas the most violent crimes like murder and rape is lead by white men but yet police profile blacks and patrol our neighborhoods. That's because police are modern day slave catchers and the prisons are the plantations. The 70% of white men are convicted of crimes, Only 35% of them do jail time. That's only half and most cases are violent crimes. January 12, 2019 in Asheville Mall, North Carolina. A 51 year old 250 pound white man name David Steven Bell punch, knocking out an 11 year old black girl during an altercation that was caught on camera. David was arrested and plead guilty to assault on a child under 12 years of age. David received no jail time only a $ 530 court fine, And have to attend anger management and racial justice workshop for 90 days. A up-state New York bus driver name Shane Piche raped a 14 year old girl in his house in July of 2018 then was arrested in September of 2018. Judge James P. Clusky only sentenced Shane Piche an 26 year old pedophile, probation for 10 years and $1,750 in court fines. While only registering him as a level one sex offender. Lyle Burgess a 79 year old white retired business man raped a 5 year old child and was only sentenced to 90 days probation on house arrested in his gated community in California. Where as a 15 year old black boy name Davis gets 5 years in jail for stealing a pair of Nike sneakers with no record of prior arrest in his name. In Lawrence Kansas a young black man Albert Wilson was charged for rape and sentenced to 12 years in prison with life probation convicted by an all white jury in 2018. But he was never proven of rapping this 17 year old white girl. Albert only admitted to kissing this white girl, there was no DNA or any other proof that this young black man had sexual intercourse with this young white harpies but yet he was sentenced over ten years in jail with no prior history of ever being arrested with a chance of being imprisoned for the rest of his life, if he ever violates his parole or they accuse him of doing so. You know how that goes for our people. Alvin Kennard was given life in prison in 1983 for stealing $ 50 from a bakery. He was finally released from his slavers after serving 36 years in slavery. And he is considered one of the lucky ones. These are but a small fraction of the difference in law between whites and black people in America. But what do you expect from an race of people that doesn't respect or see you as human when they label us 3/5 of an human being and savages that is written in their very own constitution of bill of rights. Once slavery was officially over in 1865. slavery name changed in to the black code laws. All southern states practice this law including some northern states, states like New York city, Illinois, Ohio and Michigan. The states would restrict employment for black people and if it was found out you didn't have work you was deem a criminal, If you didn't have housing you was deem a criminal and just like today criminals go to prison to work slave labor. 1866 black codes was abolish and turned in to Jim crow laws that restricted where black people can go and do which included the infamous Sundown laws where it was pretty much accepted to lynch a black person if you catch them in your town at nightfall, And yes lynching is still accepted till this very day. The police and media calls them suicide these days. Black people have the lowest rate of suicide in this country. Because most of us are scare of death and don't want to burn in hell. black people don't hang themselves because were afraid it's to painful, black people practice escapism with weed, Alcohol and partying that's how we cope with hardship. Suicide is a white/Asian person thing period. My black people slavery still exist in this country and we must band together and get rid of the accept part of the 13th amendment. Freedom is freedom and if they don't grant it then we have to be willing to take it. We can't just wait for a black messiah to come and free us, we have to do that our selves, No one person can do that, No matter how great he or she is, But together, united, Not all of us because they are too many coons and coonets who are willing to stab us in the back like they did to Martin luther king Jr, Malcom X and the Black Panther party. No, No, not all of us. Just a strong amount of real sista's and brotha's will get it done. We have to stop the white supremist from continuing to force us and our children in to slavery. The only way to do this is to be rid of this cowardness spirit that the white man has imbedded in to our souls, we can't no loner be scare to make a stand because we don't want to lose anything or afraid to die. If we don't stand for ourselves, then why would anybody else.

Chapter Three

SELF HATE/ COLORISM

Self hate and colorism is the biggest problem we have among ourselves in the black community. There's not a single black person who wasn't affected by self hate or colorism at one point in their lives. Both of these are a form of mental slavery that was inbedded in us going back to the old slavery days. If you read the Willie Lynch letter you will understand how the slave master purposely pitted light skin blacks against the darker skin tone black people. Many of the lighter skin black people were servants/ slaves inside the big house(master house on the plantations.) Even lighter skin tone men was giving so called better positions like overseer over the field working black people. Whipping them, Revealing plans and secrets that they hide from their white suppressors. Even I as a child was affected by self hatred and colorism and didn't even realized it. I am your typical brown skin colored, I wouldn't be considered dark or light skin among the black community. My father is a darker skin black man and so was his father and mother both whom I dearly loved before they departed this world. So I never thought that dark skin wasn't beautiful when I was young. But I too when I was around six to eight thought that white was the beauty standard of the world and if they were black they had to look like Lisa Bonet who played Denise Huxtable, Jasmine Guy who play whitley and Cree Summer who played Freddie on the Different World. Basically mulatto looking woman I was attracted too at that time. I remember I saw a dark brown girl on an S-curl commercial and I said out loud to myself that she was beautiful and my mother and late grandmother Ruth shouted out "O' my god the boy like black girls!". You have to understand that white and very light skin girls/ women were heavy promoted on tv, they were considered the standard of what beauty was supposed to be, Things like that influence the thinking of the youth even till this day, How many people think that Beyonce and Cardi B is the embodiment of beauty, Why you think the kardashans are so loved and famous, White girls with the thick bodies of a black sister. So how colorism works, The lighter skin you are the better looking you are, that's because knowing it or not you are saying the lighter/ whiter you are the better you look. This is another reason why black people bleach their skin to look less black and more white. How many times have you heard a black person say that a guy or girl " looks good for a dark girl or guy." or "it's to hot to be around black folks" These are all forms of colorism which now leads me to the self hatred in the black community. Self hatred runs deep inside our black community. First I will start with the men. This goes back till the civil rights days when people legally could have interracial relationships with white woman. To finally be able to touch and have sex with the white mans woman after hundred of years having the white man parade and violate their black women. It was pay back time for some black men but then you had the brothers who actually believed that white women were better because they were white, that they were smarter, not as loud or nagging like the black woman was, oh I can't forget more kinky in the bedroom, white woman were willing to do all types of nasty things in the bedroom. For a black man to dominate a white woman better then a white man can was and still is a honor for them. Where you think the phase "once you go black you won't never go back" comes from, it was about black men sexually dominating the white mans woman. Black men would also marry these white woman and have children with them hoping that now they would be part of the white family. Hoping him and his kids would be more accepted in to white sociality. Becoming coons against black sociality and blaming the black woman of being hood rats, gold diggers and black whores who have multiple babies daddies while leeching off of welfare and child support in turn believing the white woman is smarter, faithful and more supporting then black woman. Which are all lies, yes those things are true about some black women but the same is true for white women too. White women have multiple babies fathers, white woman live off of child support and welfare. Believe it or not there are more white people on welfare then black people in the United States of America. Research it yourself and see. Don't you know that black woman lead in college graduation rates in America. That alone shows how educated and smart our black sisters are. Although there have been many cases of white woman false accusing black men of rape including famous athletes, It would seem that putting their life and career on the line is worth it to them. The fact that they are willing to take those chances shows how much you hate your melanin that makes you a black man. Most coons can't stand the color of their skin so they swirl with the white woman so their children won't come out looking as black as them. These are both self hatred and colorism that have effected the black man till this very day. Now for all my black women out there. There is a lot of self hate among our sisters unfoutunately. For starters let start with the hair. Most black woman don't believe they have good hair unless it's long and straight which resembles the white woman. Which follows those who are mixed with other cultures in their blood, how they love to brag, saying "I have Indian or Spanish in my family.' It's hard as hell to get most black woman to wear their natural hair out in their natural state, Even if she has a lot of hair, She would have to wear a wig, a weave or have to perm their hair. (black men used to do this too. God bless my grandmother Ruth but she stayed trying to perm my hair and yes Jerry curls count as a perm, you just adding some black flavor on a white thing) All those chemicals eating away at your hair, Damn things be burning the hell out of the scab of your head. Hair falling off if you don't keep up with it, while still slowly eating away at your hair the more you perm it. All this trouble to have straight hair like white Becky over there and continues to go to Asian beauty stores to buy white/Asian weaves no matter how much the Asian man beat the hell out of you in their stores. You would even fight the black men in your community who are trying to boycott these Asian stores and shut them down. Most black woman would part take in these Asian beauty shops then rather shop and support an black beauty shop from their own people, because of the belief that whatever is non-black is better mindset. A black woman with her pure natural hair out is one of the most beautiful things to see in this world. That always resonated with me. Another thing I notice about a lot of my black sista's, they hate the thought of getting darker. I can't even count how many times I heard a black woman complain that their complexion is getting darker in the sun. How they would use coco butter to try to lighten their skin or how our woman are bleaching there skin in large numbers now (mostly our African, Caribbean sisters). Woman who are black, Dark brown, Brown, Tan or any other shade of black you are, you're beautiful the way you are, STOP IT! Stop trying to look like these Susan and Beckie's out here. Don't you know you black woman are on the top of the pyramid of beauty, why do you thank all these Kardashians have all these surgeries to have these full figures just like you, how they are black fishing online now making their skin darker, Braiding their hair so they can look like you. Just like the movie GETOUT. A lot of white woman hate you because they can't be you! Understand this and be the black queens you're all meant to be. Now I must talk about my Afro Latino's and Latina's out there. I'm not addressing the white Latin people out there that look like Jennifer Lopez who considered themselves white when they come over here from Puerto Rico, Cuba and other Caribbean islands. If you think you're white then damn it you're white then, and I will treat you as such. I don't believe in that one drop rule where white and other groups of people can turn around and claim black when it benefits them, Get the hell out of here with that crap! This is relating to my tan, brown and black Latin people out there who when we ask you are you black because you are to dark to claim your Spanish white heritage say's I'm 100% Puerto Rican, or Dominicano. I'm sorry no you're not, first of all Puerto Rican, Dominican, Cuban, Mexican (No forget the Mexicans part because most of you are straight white supremist like the Neo Nazi groups.) are nationalities. That's like me saying I'm 100% American. You are black, you have melanin in your blood. You are the decedents of enslave black people who were rape and torture by Spain colonies throughout the Caribbean's. You can thank Christopher Columbus for that. That's why you speak Spanish just like we speak English. our white masters were the English from England and yours was the Spanish from Spain. That's not your original language, that's broken Spanish you speak, just like I speak broken English our original language is gone just like our names. Wake up my Afro Latin people! We are all black that have the names and language of our slave masters that enslave and rape us hundreds of years ago. You afro-Latin's that can't past as white and get your white privilege cards need to get on board and join the black liberation by identifying yourself as black people. Because if black Americans/ Foundational Black Americans lose this war against white supremacy guest who's next on the list.

Chapter Four

ETHNIC/BLACK CLEANSING

This is not a theory my black people, this is a fact and it has been going on for hundreds of years as the white people claim the world with their white supremacy system. Before I get deep in to the ethnic cleansing which means to be rid of a certain race. The white supremist lust after our black people, They wish to dominate us totally by body, mind and soul you understand. The slave master would rape his slaves, female and male. That's right, sometimes the white male slave master would rape a strong black male in front of his family while making the rest of the plantation look on. It was called Bucking and Buck Breaking. Beside the white supremist gay lust for black men it was another way to break the spirit and foundation of the black family, Especially the black woman. She would watch the man she loved, the protector of her family being broking down, Sub coming in to another man's sexually well. A black woman's seeing her husband's man hood being stripe away right in front of her and their children, Image the hopelessness this installs in the black family. She would now watch over her son's, Taking away the sons warrior's spirit so he won't get in to trouble because she would fear for his manhood and his life. It was her job to make sure her son was as obedient as possible in order to please her white master. She couldn't trust the black man to protect them anymore so she did what she could to make sure their little boys didn't have any fangs so white master wouldn't have no reason to fear her little boys and force harm on to them because he was intimidated of what they could grow up to be. This was how the white man showed his dominance over the black family. The white man has a greater lust for the black woman. The slave master would rape their female slaves and they would bare him children but they wouldn't be acknowledge as such. Sometimes when their black/ mulatto daughters would grow older usually around teenage age, their slave masters/ fathers would have sex with them as well. Forcing their black daughters to bare his grandchildren. This wasn't considered incest to most slave masters because they didn't look at them as real family, Just live stock. Sometimes the master's black daughter would have to endure being rape by many slave masters at the same time when there was a party in her slave master/ father quarters that night. Such was the fate for some mulattoes black woman in those days in the big house. Sometimes even the white woman would rape black slaves mostly men, but women as well. At this time most field black man who was enslaved hated white people they knew who the enemy was. The black man would have no choice to give in to the command of their master's wife. If they didn't she would say he tried to rape her, which meant a horrific death. If you get caught by the overseer or slave master you face the same fate as she would of yelled rape. If the black man had unfoutunately impregnate her, she will be sent away and someone will snitch on you so they won't be blame by the white master. Having sex with a white woman in those days was like a horror movie, Black men of today should learn from the past. As the white woman still howls rape, Especially with the Me-too# movement going on. Because a white person have children with you and marries You, doesn't mean they love you, It doesn't mean they aren't racist. If your husband is having sex with you and calls you a Nigger Bitch it's not a kinky role play he's a racist. If you or your kids piss him/her off for whatever reason and he/she calls you a Nigger or Kaffir he/ she is a racist. If he/ she have long conversations with you how black people are racist and need to stop blaming the white man, He/She is a racist. Just like the Proud Boys an white supremacy group right here in new York city. A white supremist name John kinsman who is married to a black woman and have two children by her. She's a dark skin black woman too not a mulatto, you understand. A white supremist who killed two unarm black people in Kroger store in Kentucky name Gregory A.Bush who was stop by a black man name Dominiic Rozier. Gregory ex-wife was a black woman who he abused calling her Nigger, NiggerBitch. Even our own Halle Berry first baby daddy Gabriel Aubrey called her a nigger, while trying to erase what little blackness their daughter have inherent from Halle Berry genes. We are nothing but sexual toys for their dirty desires. Ethnic cleansing is being done right now, right here in the united states of America. Just like they doing to our brother and sisters in Brazil. Like they already done in Australia by taking the native black people children's away from them, forcing the youth to breed with only white people, and so would their children erasing pretty much whatever black genes in them by the third generation. This is not including the mass murder of the original blacks of that land, as they play a game where you plant a black child in the ground/sand and see how far you can kick their heads off. In America you can't force breed anything, Most of the black race would be dead before that happens. Whatever you may think at lest for right now America don't want that, who would be their slaves if everybody was white, they sure as hell don't want to do that kind of work. There be a civil war real quick if poor whites had to do the cheap labor we do in prison, the elite would have a hell of a fight on their hands. No,No you have to keep the poor whites busy with abusing us black folks. If you haven't notice on television shows, commercial and ads, Even our protest to the flag of America and racist star spangled banner song. Are shown with black and white couples, not black and Asian or black and Arab, differently not black on black. There are promoting black and white couples. In order to inspire to swirl white, Eliminating black families. Creating more mulatto children who may pamper more towards their white side. Look at Colin Kaepernick who got all this media attention in the league for his protest, did you know he wasn't even the first one to do so in his own league. Marshawn Lynch was doing it years before kaepernick but no one cared. No media attention at all. My opinion is he's to black, it's easier to deal with a mulatto who can feel foe their white side, then make that person the face of the movement. Don't be fooled, Stop swirling and make black families the face of black America. Because if we don't 40-50 years down the line, the offspring of mulattoes will be the new white while the black race will be a decline one. Unfoutunately breeding us out and murdering us in the streets like rapid dogs are not the only way white supremacy is trying to wipe us out with. White supremacy has now weaponize vaccines to depopulate the black race. Their main weapon is the MMR (measles, mumps, rubella) vaccines that given between one and three year old's can give your children autism. Especially if you have boys. Black boys are affected by autism 236% percent more than white children. This was stated by Dr. William Thompson who was senior lead scientist over the CDC (center for disease control) vaccine division. You see this is biological warfare and in war there are casualties. White supremacy is willing to sacrifice some of their children's future in order to depopulate and stop future birthrates of the black race. This method of warfare is very personal to me. Not just because the threat of extermination of my people but this tool of biological warfare has hit me hard. To have your seed, your legacy, your bloodline annihilated from existence is an modern form of castration. Hearing your child saying Mom and Dad, How so many of us take those simple but so beautiful words for granted as parents every day. Only to never hear your child utter those words again because you took them to get vaccinated. Only to hope but know there's more then an 90% percent chance your child would never speak again. Never have an conversation about how their day went. Too never play sports or play videogames. Never to date or fall in love. Too never marry or have children of their own. Your entire bloodline ended by three vaccine shots, two to the arm, one to the leg. Most high up's CDC scientist don't vaccinate their children because they now these shots ain't good for their children. Especially if their child is black. But here we are lining our children up for the slaughter. Not a wake about how far white supremacy will go to genocide us all. But I still have some hope left, mainly when your child is still young between the ages of two and three when the changes start to happen. As the years a by and your small baby becomes a teenager near adult hood your hope becomes grief and depression. Thoughts start to get real dark, real fast. I am not a weak minded man, Never was but at times I could be an very cold hearted person. I am an family man, I love my wife and children, having them with me is the only thing that's keep's me breathing in this world without exiting in an bath covered in crimson red blood of my enemies before they rid me of this world with their machines and gadgets. Don't think that because I'm not abandoning my family with blind rage of bloodlust, sacrificing my life by obliviating an vaccine lab or taking out some slave patrollers that I'm not angry. No I am angry and ' Anger is good because anger gets shit done!' and I am very angry. Writing this book in order too wake up my people is only the beginning of my wrath against white supremacy. Black family's, Especially the black man, is the LGQBT movement which is also known as the alpha bet people community. Now don't get me wrong I am not a homophobe because number one I have no fear of gay people and second I don't hate gay people because I have some in my very own family and have gay friends. What a grown man and woman decide who they want sexual access too is their business, it's their choice and I respect that regardless if I agree with it or not. If the LGQBT left it as that I wouldn't have a problem with it but when you involve children that's another matter, Especially black children. There is a heavy push of promotion with this LGQBT movement in the black community among our children. Cartoons where a black boy have to male parents, a black boy wearing a dress in a new children's book. A gay alphabet book made for children where a black boy is the only cross dresser gay boy. Little gay boy being flamboyant in gay parades around grown ass men, twerking and switching their 10 year old asses better then some grown ass women. But you don't see no little white boys being promoted in this life style, you don't see little white boys being gay in children books do you? No! I answer that, No you don't. Children are being told in public grade school that they no longer can be identify as being a boy or girl. If a black kindergarten see's a sparkly bag he might want to grab it because the colors are beautiful and attractive, when in the past a teacher or parent will tell that boy no pocket books are for girls, now they would put a dress on the boy and say see he wanted the pocket book so he identifies as a girl. Get the hell out of here he's 5 years old he doesn't know anything about sexual identify. This is use mainly in black public schools to indoctrinate the youth in too the LGQBT movement, Decline to stop our birth rates by opening our black youth in to pedophile, having our children corrupted before they turn the age of 12. Don't believe me what about our late great elder and queen Dr. Frances Cress Welsing who quoted in her book named the Isis Papers. "Black psychiatrists must understand that whites may condone homosexuality for themselves, But we as blacks must see it as a strategy for destroying black people, that must be countered. Homosexuals or Bisexuals should neither be condemned nor degraded, as they did not decide that they would be so programmed in childhood. The racist system should be held responsible. Our task is to treat and prevent its continuing and increasing occurrence." welsing said and continued to preach until her dying day, trying to wake up black people to the race war we are in. The more of our children that are Gay and Transsexual the less our birth rates goes up. We must protect our black children by home schooling them or protecting them from sexual pedophile's who identify as the opposite sex so they can have public access to your children. You black grown ass men that supposed to be straight that wearing dresses, appearing like woman because it's supposed to be hot, have some damn common sense, Wake the hell up! There is a race war going on and we're already losing before we realize we're in a fight. Wake up my black people or Die!

Chapter Five

STOP FORGIVING THESE WHITE SUPREMIST

Black people we have to stop forgiving these white supremist out here that are doing harm to our people. This is a form of mental slavery that our people are still suffering through and we have to break this cycle if we are going to be able to liberate ourselves. This forgiveness of the white man has been imbedded in us from the plantation days of slavery. White supremacy has weaponize christianity against us by making us believe that Jesus Christ was a white man. Many of you Christians would say it doesn't matter what color Jesus is, And I would say you are wrong absolutely wrong, it totally matters. Because when you see God or Jesus if you believe they are one in the same, you will subconsciously see white people as a reflection of god, therefore seeing them as your superior. If a white man beats you, rape you, rape your spouse and children, kill and torture your people and say that they are superior then you because god made them in his image, Then tell you to forgive them because white Jesus tells you to forgive your earthly masters. Since god, Jesus looks just like your slave masters. You will start to believe you are less then because why would god come in a form that was inferior right. Now you will pray to this white god to liberate you from his white chosen people that don't know what they do so forgive, forgive them lord for they don't know what they do. We say and teach this to our kids. Forgive, Forgive the white's because we sure in hell don't forgive each other that's for sure. We'll damn a brother or sister that does us wrong. We'll fight, kill each other real quick. It could take years to forgive a black brother or sister for just stealing from us or sleeping with our man or woman. With the younger generation you can be shot dead for stepping on their sneakers or looking at them a certain way. But with white people after years of murder, Abuse and rape we can just forgive them. They can call us niggers and the next day I forgive them. Murder your children and here you go saying I'm a christen and god said forgive so I forgive. Shit makes me sick, this is one of the main reasons we don't get no respect from any of these other nonwhite groups because we don't stick up for ourselves against these devils because of our cowardness. Don't believe me I'll give you some real life examples of brainwash, forgiving negros forgiving their white masters for things they shouldn't be forgiving for. Lets start with a situation that started in another racist state of Minnesota where a Muslim African woman name Asma Jama was talking to a friend of hers in Swahili, A white racist name Jodie marie Burchard-Risch approach this young woman and busted a beer mug across her face. Asma had to get medical attention with cuts to her mouth, chest and hands from the shattered glass that was smash across her face. The day of the court sentencing the Muslim woman ask to speak to the racist white woman. Before Asma could start speaking she began to cry a little bit saying to herself "I don't want to do this." she struggle on saying "she don't know what's wrong with her today, she's usually stronger than this." she said. I know what was wrong with her, her spirit was dying inside screaming for justice, trying to fight off the cowardness that was imbedded in us by the white man's religion, yes I know she's a Muslim. She then goes on and say because of her religion she forgives her. While also saying "I pray she learns from this and she can open her heart and realize that at the end of the day, we are all the same. It doesn't matter where you are form." she said While this white racist had nothing to say back to her, Jodie racist daughter sat in the court with a smirk, fighting hard not to laugh out loud in this black woman's face. These are the demons you want to forgive? If you have to forgive. Then forgive in private not in public in front of these monsters and the rest of the world to see. Do you not know you can pray to god to deliver your enemies in your hand. You can ask god to destroy those who does evil up on you, And it is righteous to do so. When the great revolutionary Nate Turner prayed for god to give him a sign to destroy his oppressors. He didn't just kill the slave masters he murder the whole damn family (yes children included.) Damn! All is being ask of you is to say, I don't forgive, May you and those like you suffer to the fullest extent of the law. Another example of this yes master sickness was in Oxford, Alabama. Kimberly Houzah was profiled by the owner of a Victoria Secret and was kicked out of the store because of some bull crap about a black female earlier stole from their store. So what, Are you saying if a white woman steals from your store you're gonna kick whatever white woman enters your store from now on too? Let me answer that "HELL NO! They won't. Kimberly protest against the store and it became national news. The owner of Victoria secret apologizes to kimberly. A news reporter ask this young woman will she shop again at Victoria secret and she said. She probably will still shop at Victoria secret but, may not be at that location. My god are you blinking kidding me, why even protest. You don't even have the sense or self respect to not go back to the damn same store that profiled you. This is why they can do things to us so openly now, we are considered a blinking joke! How can black people conduct a proper boycott and shut things down, when the person you was boycotting the store for goes right back in it. Fayetteville North Carolina. At a trump rally, A black man was escorted out by the name of Rakeem Jones. He was elbow in the face by a old white supremist name John franklin Mcgraw.

Instead of law enforcement arresting this old racist bastard for assault they manhandle Rakeem and arrest him. Right after the media questioned the old racist. This man had the nerve to say "The
next time we see him, We might have to kill him." He's a old school
racist that's 79 years old, probably been to a few lynching parties
back in his days. So you knew he meant that and the crowd went
wild with excitement when this old racist assault Rakeem. During
the court date John Mcgraw was sentenced to probation. John was
force to apologizes and held out his hand, This negro shakes his
hand but he couldn't leave it at that he had to hug this man, That
Man didn't really want to hug you fool! After wards Rakeem said" It
was genuine" "Even if it wasn't what people expected him to say or
felt like he should have said, it was him all the way around." yeah
alright house negro and when he elbow you in the face that was
genuine too sense you like keeping it real. Oakland, California. A
known white supremist name John Lee Cowell ran behind two
young black woman name Nia and Letifah Wilson they were sisters.
Cowell stabbed them both in the neck killing the younger sister Nia.
She was only 18 years old. The Oakland police found the killer and
arrested him with **care.** There were protesters in the streets, black
people were trying to get things done, sick and tried of these racist
pigs who think they are superior then us, like hell they are. Nia god-
father Duryle Allums made a statement to the black people of
Oakland, saying. "We need the community especially the African
American community to stand down right now." Duryle said. This
man god daughter was just murdered by a white supremist and he's
telling black people to stand down. The cowardness of our black
people is trouble some. brothers like this can actually stop a uprising or an revolution. Duryle continues. "We're asking the community to respect the family and don't put any blood on our hands."
He finished. Don't put blood on our family hands he said, which
means that Nia father and mother shared his feeling's right. Your

little girl just got murdered in broad daylight by a known white supremist, Then he almost killed your other daughter all in one attack
and you don't want no blood on your hands. But your daughters'
blood can be spilled across the Oakland streets for all could see. I
don't respect you or your family. You are the definition of the slave
who had an opportunely to escape their white masters but were to
scare to act. Just a bunch of scared ass coons! This is why we are the
cattle and they are the predators my people. In my own backyard in
Brooklyn New York. A evil white racist name Theresa klein Falsely
accused a 9 year old boy name Jeremiah Harvey of grabbing her
butt, personal she didn't have anything to touch back there anyway
but that's just my opinion. The video footage showed that Jeremiah
book bag barley touch her and she went crazy. The she devil started
touching her flat ass in front of the boy saying he want this. Thersa
started doing sexual movements in front of him, showing what she
believes the little boy want's to do to her, which we all know it's
probably the other way around. Now all those sexual gesture she
did to Jeremiah was pedophile behavior. Now she accused the boy
of something that he didn't do, that was proven by eye witnesses
and video footage. Fifthly years ago, if this would had happened,
this could of easily been another Emmitt Till situation. You know
how many young boys and men were torture and murder because
white woman falsely accuse us brothers for looking or touching
them in some way. That's why little Jeremiah started crying when
he was falsely accused by this racist sicko. Thersa later ask the boy
for forgiveness while admitting she didn't know the boy's(Jeremiah's)
name. Jeremiah responded by saying: "I don't forgive this woman,
And she needs help" he said. When I heard that, I was like yes, yes
that's the attitude that black people have to have. This little boy
was a hero to us, especially foundation black Americans. This nine
year old boy did what grown ass men and women didn't have the
courage to do. This boy is an A plus student with the spirit of an true

great black warrior, I felt there was a change coming. Then here's comes the child's mother undermining everything. After all our people did to rally behind her and Jeremiah's cause. Someko Bellille goes on national television and say's she forgives this racist woman and don't want nothing too happened to her. Which strips away whatever power the black community was building up to pressure the new York D.A to press charges against Theresa Klein. More dishearten then that was to watch this young proudful boy with a warrior spirit.(remember what I said about mothers defanging their little boys for white supremacy.) was defang right in front of us on live television as his mother made him apologizes. The boy was struggling, you can tell he didn't want to apologizes, But he had to respect what his mother told him to do, Because it would seem that his father is not in the picture to save Jeremiah's black pride of manhood. I will admit I was piss off the whole day after watching that. Then there was the famous or infamous Rodney King who was almost beating to death by the slave patrol/cops on tape, of course the cops got away with it, Just like always when it comes down to justice against the slave patrol. Black people of California had enough of the slave patrol framing, beating, killing them in the streets and they rioted and started beating white people ass including the cops all over Oakland California. Then here comes Rodney King with that infamous speech. "Can we all get along. Can we stop making horrible for old people and the kids." he pleaded. The hell with that they should of took the fight down to Beverly Hills California and make an example of the rich white folks. Dallas Texas, A racist police officer name Amber Guyer murdered a black man named Botham Jean. Botham Jean was shot and killed in his own apartment, Unarmed sitting down on his couch in his under clothes eating ice cream watching TV. Amber Guyer busted in Botham apartment claiming she thought it was her own apartment but ignore all the signs that showed it wasn't her place. Like her electric card key didn't work on the door, there was a red carpet in front of the door that wasn't in front of her place, then clearly once Amber open up the door there was the difference in furniture arrangements. Even with all those signs she still proceeded forward and murdered Botham Jean in his own home. During the trail it was revealed how the racist Amber Guyer is by exposing some of her text messages in court. One of her fellow officers who was name "Blevin" in her texts. He wanted to know how long the Martin Luther King day parade lasted, because Amber worked the MLK parade for ten years. Amber replied: "When MLK is dead," then she finished with "Oh wait..." Also the murdering racist continues by saying he could "Spray (his) pepper spray in that general area." I guess that's her way of joking about macing innocent black people to make less attendance around him. Two months later someone text Amber: "At an area with five different black officers." adding: "I'm not racist but damn!" the person text Amber as she replied with: "Not racist but just have a different way of doing things." I guess even among the white pigs they can't stomach being around but so many coons. Two days before Amber Guyer murdered Botham Jean she received an text by some one name "Etheridge" the person offer Amber a German shepherd because their apartment was to small, But the person warned that the dog might be a little racist. Of course Amber replied with: "It's ok." "I'm the same." Amber text. So after Botham being murdered in his own apartment by an cop that was more concern about losing her job then saving the life of batham as he bleed to death proven how racist she truly was. Now to Botham Jean's coon ass family. Botham little brother said in the court room: "If you truly are sorry...I know I can speak for myself...I, I forgive you" He forgave this murdering slave catcher who clearly was only sorry because she faced real jail time. He continues: "And I know if you go to god and ask him, he will forgive you." Brandt said. But that wasn't all it get's worst. "I love you just like anyone else." "I'm not going to say I hope you rot and die, just like my brother did...I personally want the best for you." This coon ass, Plantation ass sell out just said he love's her and want's the best for her. It's sickening, thinking of this coonary make's my damn stomach hurt. This is the type of enslaved person who would stand by and watch his children be torture and lynch in front of him and won't do shit, Accept cry and pray for god to forgive them for what they done. Brandt continues his coon fest by asking the judge Tammy (the mammy) Kemp: "I don't know if this is possible, But can I give her a hug. Please." he pleaded "please." he pleaded again to the judge. Judge Kemp allowed it and these two basically ran in to each others arms and embrace each other like lost lovers who finally reunited after years of being apart. It felt like I was stuck in some kind of mess up reality like the Twilight Zones. Because of this sickening display of forgiveness Amber Guyer only was sentence to 10 years which she will only serve 5-4 years in jail for good behavior and time served. Even the damn father joins in the coonary by saying: "I'd like to become your friend at some point." This negro said in some sambo church he spoke at. Bertram and your son Brandt with the rest of your coon ass family make me sick! Because of black people like this, make's things more dangerous for us. They give the world the appearance that it's okay to murder us and won't have to worry about punishment not even the legal way. This makes law enforcement job easier to criminalize and kill us in these streets with impunity. Like Atatiana Jefferson who was shot and killed by an slave patrol officer name Aaron Dean. Who shot Atatiana through her window when she approaches the light that Dean beamed in her face before assassinating her in her own damn home on a wellness check! We have to stop forgiving these white supremist devils. we get nothing out of it but more disrespect for being so damn weak. This is why Christopher Columbus prayed on the black natives of Hispaniola because they were soft and kind, Always forgiving, they even saved their crew from a watery grave when they first arrived and all the white man did was took your kindness for weakness. For you religious black folks out there god/ Jesus wasn't a white man he was a black, If you actually read your bible and stop going by what you hear and see in church you would know that. He wasn't born on December 25th ether understand. God said to smite thy enemy, they didn't beat the etomites or philphines by just praying, They had to fight, they had to get blood on their hands. Martin luther king Jr was a great, brave man but I don't agree on everything he did with the black community. but he also did a lot of good thing as well so don't get me wrong. This enemy who has been oppressing us for hundreds of years can't be forgiving and prayed for, that won't change a damn thing. Stop waiting for god to come down to rescues you and start saving your own damn selves, Black Power to all the people. Wake the hell up my black people and stop getting in your own damn way of liberation!

Chapter Six

BEWARE OF THE COONS AND COONETS

First off I want to start off with the term Uncle Tom which got started from a novel named uncle toms cabin. Uncle tom was base off a real life man named Josiah Henson. Josiah Henson was born in to slavery in the state of Charles county Maryland, In June 15, 1789. Josiah father received 100 lashes across his back for standing up to his plantation master in front of Josiah. The overseer then pin Josiah father's right ear to the whipping post, then followed up by cutting it off before selling him off to another plantation somewhere in Alabama. Sometime after the rest of his family was sold off, his brothers and sisters were sent somewhere else as his mother was sold to a plantation owner named Isaac Riley. Josiah mother pleaded to her new slave owner too at least buy back her youngest son Josiah, and so he did. Josiah became one of his most prized slave servant. Isaac Riley promise to grant Josiah freedom for $450. Over the years Josiah managed to pay his master $350 of the $450 dollars for his freedom. When Josiah was ready to finished buying off for his freedom, Isaac Riley added an extra zero to note he gave to Josiah saying he owned $100 but change it to $1000. Josiah realized his so called master was never going to let him go. Josiah managed to escape to Ontario, Canada with his wife Nancy Henson and four children. Black people in Canada was considered free, If you managed to succeed in escaping that far avoiding white and Indian slave catchers through out the United States of America. Josiah made a safe haven for run a way enslaved men and women of the black race. Josiah also became an officer in the Canadian army leading an all black unit in the Canadian rebellion in 1837. He became an author later on in life, His first book was an autobiography of himself named "The life of Josiah Henson, Formerly a slave, Now an Inhabitant of Canada, Narrated by Himself "In 1849. This believed to inspired the novel by Harriet Beecher Stowe's Uncle Tom's Cabin in 1852. where a man named uncle tom who was born in to slavery and was a christen man. Uncle Tom was beaten for not betraying his follow slaves and for teaching chrisanity. Uncle Tom advise a mother and her daughter to escape the cruel plantation, when the master finds out he orders Tom to sell them out but he doesn't, so they beat him to death. Even as he was getting beaten to death he forgave his oppressors which changed the lives of his killers as they converted to chrisanity. Uncle Tom was considered a **Hero.** As this book became a best seller helping to spark the civil war. Abraham Lincoln met Harriet stowe he quoted saying; "So this is the lady who started the great war." Just think about that before you decide to call a sellout a **uncle Tom** again because whatever you thought of uncle Tom's actions or non actions. Was he a sell out? No, was he a forgiving submissive man? Yes. But in real life Josiah Henson was nether of those things. Now for the real Coons, which is an word short for Racoons. A large colored rat with white stripes, sounds about right to me. Also could be referred by the name Barracoon, a prison that the white supremist held us captured during the Atlantic slave trade for transportation. Coons and Coonets are the most dangerous to the black community and for black liberation. There has been many black rebellions suppressed because of coons throughout our history. Harriet Tubman and Winnie Madikizela- Mandela had zero tolerance for the coons. Harriet was willing to shoot any slave that was trying to head back to the plantation after she rescues them from slavery. Because she knew the first thing they would do was snitch, Revealing the secrets of the Underground Rail Road to their white masters. Winnie Mandela had more harsh techniques for the traders of the black rebellion by torturing and setting these coons on fire. Those were the times of true warfare for black liberation, Killing was an acceptable means of war. Before you can successfully take on white supremacy, we must first deal with the want to be white supremist in our own back yard first, The rotten **coons**. I'm not telling you to go out in kill any coons, but we must completely disown them, band their voice, exile them from the black community. There can't be no mercy, no compromise no matter who they are, Their venom can not be allow to effect the our black youth, Because if they infect our black youth on a large scale then, the war is lost. Our children and their children, children's will smile and thank our suppressors as they tie nooses around their necks, mocking us as we thank them believing we are free and these post-racism days. You know it's true we already have fools in this generation already doing this. How some black people can be so blind is beyond me. There are many modern day coons out here today. I won't be able to name them all but I'll name what I feel are the most dangerous ones here in America. Let's start with the old coons. Number one I must name the minister and public speaker Jessie lee Peterson. This coon have said out of his own mouth that "Racism doesn't exist, And never has." when I first heard this coon utter those words from his mouth I really thought it was some kind of sitcom but this was real and he was real. I believe that this 70 year old man really believes the abomination that comes from his mouth. This coon goes on around ministering this house negro stuff to whom ever are willing to hear it. This old coon also said things like. Jim crow, Racial Segregation wasn't white supremacy but laws that was made from the government. That if he could, he would have black people pick cotton again because it build good work ethic. It's hard to believe that there are white and black people out here who would listen to this man, being born and living through the civil rights movement in Alabama and preaching racism doesn't exist and believe him because they want to believe in this fake post-racism America. Another one of these old coons is the former sheriff ;David Clarke It was a good day when this coon had to step down from being sheriff of the Milwaukee county, Wisconsin police department. I would hate to know how many innocent black men and women this coon had lock up during his 37th years as a sheriff. This man had a unbelievable hatred for Black Lives Matters and deemed them as an racist hate group along with the New Black Panthers party and the Nation of Islam. This coon of course never acknowledges the murders his police officers/ slave portals done to unarmed black man and women throughout the U.S.A But this coon can consent bring up how black lives matter is an anti-cop terrorist group who are the most dangerous organization since the Ku Klux Klan. The fact this so called black man can compare the black lives matter movement to the proven murderous hate terrorist organization named the Ku Klux Klan in the same breathe is abomination too all of the black race.

Now for the coonets of the world I will start with someone I wouldn't considered a real danger to the black community but is very popular and can persuade young female minds that want to be like her. This coonet is known as Blac Chyna. The man eating self hatred popular stripper who became a celebrity dating and having Rob Kardashans child. Now she's a business woman who has sold out to a company name whiteolious that produces bleaching powder to lighting the skin of self hating black women who are dealing with the willie lynch affect of hating their black skin, believing the lighter and whiter you Are, The better you are. For an black sister to pray on her fellow dark skin sista's insecure of their beautiful melanin skin color is very low, Even for a stripper called Blac Chyna,

Who should be called white Chyna for now on. Candace Owens is the new popular conservative coonnet who is another one who believes we live in a post-racism era. Now Candance is one of these immigrants that feels like she can tell foundational black Americans about how to feel about racism and what we shouldn't get with reparations. Candace Owens being a conservative, Dr. Martin Luther King was a conservative, So was Abraham Lincoln. My problem with this sister is that she is clearly intelligent and she supports Donald Trump as president of the united states. A president who has deep ties to all-right racist organization like the Ku-Klux-Klan and neo Nazi groups. A president who refused to condemned the racist organizations in the Charlottesville Virginia attack, where a man name James Alex Fields Jr. A known Neo Nazi White supremist. Rammed his car through a crowd of protesters killing a woman named Heather Heyer, while injuring 28 other people that day. Also she went on TMZ live, when kanye west said "When you hear about slavery for 400 years, For 400 years? That sounds like a choice." Kanye West said. Right then and there Candace Ownens so called want to be leader of the new black revolution should of step in right there and corrected her partner for speaking reckless on public television. But she didn't because she's not about the causes of real black liberation. Saying things like more people get struck down by lighting then black people are killed by police. While saying we are over privilege who are complaining about things that happen to our grandparents, Who didn't complain as much. Really I couldn't believe someone who supposed to be so smart and black and liberated could say something so stupid. Didn't you see Martin Luther King protest in the streets. Marching up and down the streets of the racist south, being beating, hoes down and attack by dogs by white supremist on live television. Didn't you see the great Malcom X condemn the white man every chance he had on live television. Didn't you see the Black Panthers Party of Defense rise up to the white supremist government of the united states. Didn't you see how all these great leaders where assassinated and imprisoned in slavery by the white supremist government and their Black sellout coons of the united states of America? Did you? Yeah you did. And I know you don't truly be leave the shit you saying but you want to famous, you being the young female mammy black coonet immigrant that support the republicans along with supporting Donald Trump pretending racism doesn't exist anymore in America. You sold out because when you was talking shit about the same Donald trump when you was a liberal a year before you wasn't notice, Now all a sudden you know the errors of your ways supporting the democrats. Candace acts like leaving the liberal party for the conservative is some kind of big movement for black people, That's gonna change the world. You mammy ass coon you make me sick! Now for the final coonet on this list. Unlike the Lizzo's of the world, an woman who willingly degraded for white supremacy approval by making herself an modern day display of Sarah Baartman. This person, This woman who is black only in skin color but who's soul is whiter then the void itself. An person who is a lot more dangerous then an Lizzo or an Loni Love towards black society, is the biggest plantation Mammy in America, Oprah Winfrey. Revere to be the ideal black woman in all society, is nothing but another agent of white supremacy. I have no idea what could of happened in oprah's life that cause her to have so much disdain for black men, Betraying her own people. I first notice how oprah would play and even produce herself in black male bashing movies such as The Color Purple and Beloved where black men are portrayed to be Rapist, Pedophile's, cheats, Abusive and just good for nothing men. Now being the age I was then at the time I didn't really see what the big deal was. Yeah Oprah don't like black men but that doesn't make her a straight traitor to her people right? Yeah my question was answered with her true colors being revealed by endorsing that hit piece of an documentary called

Leaving Neverland, Slandering Michael Jackson's name after his death by two liars named Wade Robson and James Safechuck who admitted that MJ never sexual abused them when he was a live. Oprah Winfrey was suppose to be one of Michael Jackson's closest friends. But yet she never challenged their lies and went further by endorsing it. Then she goes after another famous black man name Russell simmons. Personally, I don't care for him especially after he disrespected the great Harriet Tubman's name by making an porn about her sleeping with the white slave master. A womanizer he is but an rapist, that hasn't been proven. The truth is proof but truth doesn't matter because this is all made to distract from the white rapist and pedophiles that are out here and put an black face on it. This is Oprah's real job. Because if it wasn't why haven't she speak out against her old pal Harvey Weinstein, A man who made an career of forcing sexual acts on up incoming actresses. Just like this black European woman name Kadian Noble who was introduce to Harvey by Oprah. But when Harvey force this young black woman to give him head in an bathroom, Where was Oprah out cry then? Where was Oprah to protect black women from these white predators? Oh, I guess they get the same treatment like those young black girls did in south Africa right Oprah? But as long as you protect your white pay masters and slander the black mans name, you're good with that. This entire government, Liberals, Conservative all support white supremacy. The liberals pretend they're your friends, that there to support black rights then stab you in the back with a smile on their face, telling you it's for your own good and you believe it. The conservative are usually upfront with there's. What you see is what you get unless you a black coon with a lot of money because the hell with the poor blacks or black liberation when I'm good because I'm making more than 100,000 a year with my white wife or husband. Turning a blind eye to racism until it's to late when it's your turn to be hang from the noose.

Chapter Seven

POWER OF THE BLACK FAMILY

The most important goal for the white supremacy is the destruction of the black family. Economics is a far second, But most importantly is the black family because if the black family is together, their children will follow the example of their Mother and father's. Creating unity in the black community. There is nothing more dangerous then a black man that knows what he is and know who his true enemies are, for the white supremist, for the black man will install his will and strength within his children. The enemy that is the system of white supremacy know this as well. This is when the willie lynch syndrome takes place. The white supremist knew to break up the black family was to destroy the image of the black man in front of the black woman and their children. For if you disempower the black man in front of the black woman, she could no longer depend on the man/ the father of her children to be the protector of the family any longer, it was now her responsibly to protect their offspring. I discussed some of this in an earlier chapter. The white supremist would grab two of the most strong respected black men in the plantation. Then have their woman and child watch as the slave master would take the strongest of the two, Beat him in front of his family sometimes burn him as well. Then the slave masters would tie the black man down and violate him with objects up his anal, Or just straight anal rape him in front of his family. Then strap each of his legs to a horse, hitting the horse behind causing it to run separate ways ripping the black man insides apart, killing him. The second black man is whipped until a inch of his life but is kept alive, breaking his will to escape or to fight back, Damning him forever to be a servant to his white master. Seeing a grown black man who was respected throughout the plantation and have the man's wife witness such horror breaking her spirit of ever believing a black man could ever protect her and their children. The woman without the man presence would now teach her son to obey everything the white man says in order to live, And if she has a daughter she will teach her to obey and to teach her brothers and her children the same. Therefore the black boy's warrior spirit is broken before he turns 16 years old. While his sister and mother take charge of things in order to keep such a fate that happened to their fathers from happening to their black young sons. Now a young black man will grow up cowardly, Needing the woman to take charge, feminize, strong grown man who doesn't know how to become a man, because no matter how strong a woman is, she could never teach a man how to be a man. A man raised only by a woman can't truly teach a man to be a man as well. Therefore, the structure of the black family is destroyed. Founturnately some black men learned to hide their hatred in front of the white man and taught their young boys to become strong black men in secret. But the damage has been done to the black family, while the white supremist isn't done destroying the black family till this day. During the 60[ties] in the black power movement, when black people where united like they never been before in the united states of America. We were proud to be black men and women in those days. From our clothes to our beautiful natural hair. We were black and proud. We were an problem for the white supremist from Martin Luther King, Malcom X and the Black Panther Party, The white supremacy system was in deep jeopardy because no matter what leaders we had, That they killed. there were others willing and ready to take their place for black liberation. There was an uprising coming and their slave patrol tactics wasn't going to stop us. So they came up with a plan to poison us, just like how the Japanese conquer the Chinese, They flooded us with drugs. The beginning of the crack epidemic. This is the era that I grew up in. I don't know a person who wasn't touch by the crack epidemic in the 1980's and early 1990's. I couldn't walk down the street in the south Bronx without seeing those colorful crack tubes/ bottles whatever the hell you wanted to call it back then. Abandon buildings that was now used as crack houses. Which allowed all kinds of things to happen inside there, I know. I've been in a few looking for family member's as a kid with my grandfather, who raised me to be the man I am today. With so many broken homes in the black community, Again because of crack, the white supremacy won again. The black revolution was over, we couldn't fight the system when we were too busy trying to survive the streets as our mothers, fathers, aunts, uncles smoked their life away on those glass pipes. Lets not forget the ware fare system was also made to break up the black family. Mainly to keep the father out of the home, help the black woman to feel more dependent on the white man. Free money to bare children but you can't have a man live in your house, and can't receive gifts or money from him or you would be cut off. Black women would have their baby fathers sneak in to the house at night to have their personal time, so she won't lose her benefits. And because the woman is now the dominated person in the house hold, If the black man try's to install his thoughts on how their kids should be raised, she has complete domain to kick him out of the house or make it hard for him to see his kids. There for creating a dysfunction black family. The little boy will grow up dogging women, not having the will of a true man to raise his family becoming a dead beat dead. Or becoming the **sissy** of the family scared to speak and stand up for himself or his kids if he believes his woman is doing wrong by them. This is what black people call **simps.** Without an real family structure in the black family sometimes when a man is raised only by women they come out more feminized. This is by design to feminized black men, to make them less threating for the white supremist. The white supremist knows if the black liberation is to succeed you have to have strong black men as leaders of the movement. Another example of how the white supremist tries to destroy the black family is to encourage abortions in the black community. Always encouraging our black women to get their tube tied once you have a child. Especially if you're young in age, talking about that you throwing away your life or future. Now as a teen you don't even need a parent consent to abort their unborn child. The federal government a long with the help of Dr. Martin Luther King approved the abortion pill that was later called the "**Pill**" many other pro black leaders like Angela Davis supported it as well. Just like I explained before interracial relationships between whites and blacks are heavy promoted. This all done to slowly cleanse the black gene, Using your own self hate to destroy our selves. Us as the black man must restore our image to the black woman. We must show them that they can depend on us, that we are willing and able to protect and provide for them and our children. We as black men have to become leaders and providers of the black family again. We as black men cannot run away because the black women seem to be harder on us black men then their oppressors. We must rise to challenge and help heal our black women. The black woman had endured so much damage from the white supremist, the way they treat us black men is a straight result of the willie lynch symptom that pledge the black community for hundreds of years. This is why they look at the oppressor with more favor then us. Think about it, Look how the white man support our woman. The white man helps the black woman by providing her and her children with benefits on welfare while you aren't a round, they pay their rent, provide food and help them punish you with child support when you aren't taking care of your kids. The white supremist says look how I provide while your black men are to busy hustling and screwing every stripper and Instagram model they can find while you struggle at home taking care of his kids. Of course that's not true for all black men, just like it's not true that all black women depend on the white man's welfare system. There are more white people on welfare in the united states of America than any other group of people. But this is the image that has been branded on us. Our women might nag, complain just straight up give us a hard time, But if we do what we supposed to do, And show them that we can stand our ground as real black men, A black woman will respect you, And theirs no woman more loyal then an real black woman. **The black family equals black unity and black unity is the true threat to destroy white supremacy.**

Chapter Eight

WE HAVE NO FRIENDS

I need for black people to understand, Especially foundational Black Americans we have no friends in this world. All we have is our selves, All we can trust is our selves and even then you can't trust everyone who have the same skin color as yourself. I've touch on some of this earlier in this book but now I am fully going in on this topic. As an foundational black American we are in the front lines inside the belly of the beast in America fighting against the strong arm of white supremist in this world. First the Native Americans should be talked about first since many black people manly foundational black Americans act like having Native American blood is some kind of badge of honor. I can't count how many times through my life I heard my people say especially the women I have good hair or light skin because I have Indian in my blood, or I have Indian in my family. Did you know that native Americans enslaved us along with the white supremist? That the Cherokee Indians were the largest group of slave masters within the native American tribes. Now think about that, for all you black people who brag that you had Cherokee in your blood. Think how your black family had obtain this Native American blood, was it by choice? I highly dought that, Most likely your great, great, great grandmother was rape by an Indian to get you your so call light skin and good hair. An black person who was enslave by the Indians are called Freedman. So if you ever heard or hear an Native American use this term, Their talking about black people who they enslaved or their mocking you by calling you an freedman. Native Americans fought alongside with the south in the civil war because they wanted to keep us enslaved did you know that? I too have native American in my family's bloodline, Trust me it's nothing I'm proud of. My grandfather's mother was an full blooded Native American who married a black man and had two sons and three daughters. I've spoken to her a few times when I was a child, She was a beautiful person, she had an very nice and sweet soul. When she died and I saw her at her funeral, I've notice I didn't see no Native Americans there. I'm pretty sure all you black people who love and endure your Indian blood haven't met one Native American in your family haven't you? There is an reason for that, one, It's because your ancestors were their slaves or because an native American willingly step out and had an real relationship with your black grandmother or father and was cast out by the rest of their Indian family. So please especially my Foundational Black Americans stop bragging about these people who never gave a damn about you and still don't till this very day and be proud that you are an Black American. Second on this list is the Asian Community. How many of you experience going to an corner store that an Asian person owns and have that Asian person follow you around or tell you to hurry up and buy. As an black kid growing up in new York city in the late eighties and early nineties I've experience firsthand a lot. These Asians will open up their corner stores, fruit stands liquor stores, fast food restaurant with god knows what those chicken & broccoli, sesame chicken and spare ribs are really made of and nail salons in our community taking money from us while building their community's as they call us stupid black monkeys or niggers behind our backs, Damn sometimes right in our faces (manly black single women). Don't you know in their country's china, japan and Korea they have and sell sambo dolls (Jim crow dolls that are black with big red lips with big buck eyes.) they even have signs saying no blacks. They have commercials and poster ads with black face in plan view. Remember how the Asians attack our women when they were alone without an black man beside their side. Wake up people Asians don't like you they despises you! Then they are the Latin people. The fake Brown And Black Alliance. How many (brown) people have you seen stand up for black rights when we were and still being shot down in the streets of the United States of America for all to see. But yet they expect you to protest and fight putting your life on the line for immigrants that are crossing over to America illegally. I say hell no! Let them handle their own business just like they let us handle ours when one of our people gets murdered in the streets. Did you know that most Latin people that voted, voted for Donald Trump. Now their facing the consequences of their actions. you know that many Latin people join the slave patrol too make good with white supremacy. Abusing us with their fellow white masters. The racist officer named Alejandro Giraldo in south Florida abuse an black woman name Dyma Loving who called the police because an white supremist pulled out an shotgun on her and her friend and threaten to shot the "burnt black ass face off her neck." instead of interrogating the man who pull the gun on them, He instead harassed Dyma Loving until she got frustrated with the cop's stupid questioning then the racist bastard decides to manhandle her by putting her in an headlock arresting her for no reason, when it was her that called for help. Another case recently is an slave patroller named Christopher Martinez who beaten a young black boy that was 17 years old named London Wallace with multiple punches to the head that drew blood from his face when he wasn't even fighting back. Now Wallance is suing the Fresno Police Department in California. These are but an small example that the Latin Community's isn't with us. Not only do they stand against us in law enforcement but through politics and social media as well. Example Texas senator Ted Cruz who supported the actions of Amber Gayger an white Dallas police officer who shot and killed a black man in his own damn apartment by claiming she thought it was her own apartment. Ted Cruz stated on live television that Democrats were. "Quick to always blame the police officer." which we all know is for show Democrats and Republicans both don't give a damn about black lives especially those who are Foundational Black Americans. Then he continues by saying "It may well be that two lives were destroyed that night." Cruz said. Really only White Supremist can make the murder who shot and killed an innocent black man in his own apartment look like a victim. So were supposed to be sad for her killing an innocent man because she could lose her job and possibly do jail time. This how little our lives mean to these people. He continues "That obviously the individual that was at home in his apartment and found himself murdered- that is horrific and a nightmare." sometimes it's hard to believe the crazy stuff that these white supremist will say to excuse their actions. This mother Fker said he "Found himself murdered." who the hell finds themselves murdered, you don't wake up one morning and be like oh, I have bullet holes in my damn chest today, like you found some lost socks that disappeared last weekend. No your fellow white supremist she devil force her way in to this innocent man's apartment and murdered him in cold blood. He also added "She may have been in the wrong and if a jury of her peers believes that she behaved wrongly then she'll face the consequences. But I don't think we should jump to conclusions." He said. By that statement you would think Ted is talking about convicting her for jail time for murder right? Like Amber said it was an accident she thought it was her own apartment. (Bullshit by the way but let's go with that to be fair.) No this was an argument about her getting fired, Not jail time, but don't jump to conclusion's because she could lose her job for killing an unarmed man in his own apartment that she thought was her own and she shouldn't lose her job because of that. You see the con here? He's making it sound like Amber losing her job is equal to this innocent black man name Botham Jean losing his life. So if she gets off and she lose her job in the process the black community will feel like their were some kind of justice was done, Like the case with Eric Gardner, when slave patrol officer Daniel Pantaleo who put Gardner in an illegal chokehold killing him in public on camera and still got off with no jail time but finally got fired five years later after Gardner's murder, The cops all cried foul and did their little protest like losing an city job equals to an black man's life. Knowing all Daniel Pantaleo have to do is go across the bridge in the next city and he will be working again as an police/slave patrol officer soldiering on for the glory of white supremacy. Then you have other's who like to pretend they're with us and back stabs the black community the first chance they get while telling you their doing what's best for you, like this pretender name Coleman Cruz Hughes an twenty three-or four year old man who declares himself as Puerto-Rican until his career wasn't lifting off like he wanted, so he started calling himself African-American. This man someway-somehow was invited to an meeting about reparations for Foundational Black Americans too speak on our behalf. The whole reparations meeting was a scam for the H.R-40 bill. An nothing bill that's made to study if foundational black Americans should get reparations. After 400 years of cattle slavery and Black codes, Red lining, Jim crow and modern day slavery conducted by the prisons complex, Were every other group in the united states legal and illegal get tangibles over us. Acting like this bill could make a difference, While also opposing the bill at the same time, in order to control the narrative. It's all an big trick bag of shit. But anyway this pretender argues that "If we were to pay reparations today, we would only divide the country further, Making it harder to build the political coalitions required to solve the problems facing black people today." this sellout said. I haven't heard no one said that about the Jews getting reparations. Shit my taxes help pay for that shit and America had nothing to do with their Holocaust. What about the Native Americans reparations, what about the Japanese reparations, No, nothing to say? What about a bill to discuss if they deserve reparations like the H.R.-40 bill? No they can just get it. Didn't 9-1-1 families just got approve for reparations. Where was all this energy when the LGQBT just got approve for some form of cash reparations. Where was the cry out then? I guess not since you like swinging on poles in the New York City subway trains in your underwear while taking photo shots and making rap songs about how your dick is nice and you only mess with white dudes. Guess that explains it all huh Coleman Cruz, Hughes. Now and finally the most harmful backstabbing group within the black community is the Caribbean and African immigrants in this country that sabotage our progress every chance they get. Understand this doesn't relate to all black immigrants. There are induvial that are about real black unity and power for all black people but as an group, as an group they seek the downfall of Foundational Black Americans. Understand that most black immigrants don't look at us as the same. When foundational black Americans hang with black immigrants, we called them brothers and sisters we didn't indifferent ourselves from them, we considered all melanin people the same, Black. Most Immigrants don't see themselves as black first. When someone ask them what are they, the first thing they say is their Jamaican, Barbados, Kenyan or Nigerians. Their allegiants are to their tribes or mother nations. Then a lot of them will come over to this country and crap on us while using the resources that foundational black Americans fought hard for in this country. I 've lived in Harlem for eleven years and I remember when I went by an African restaurant they had a sign on their window saying ' We are not blacks we are Africans. They are not us.' They perceive us, Foundational Black Americans as inferior, lesser then them, Especially the Africans who have special names for us F.B.A. Like the word ' AKATA' and cotton pickers. When I was younger I never understood why Africans would act differently towards F.B.A. But yet treat the white man with such respect. You have to understand that many west African nations was involve in the slave trade especially the Nigerians. Till this very day they are proud of their heritage of slave traders and catchers, I'll give you a few examples: The New Yorker wrote an article about an Nigerian woman name Adaobi Tricia Nwaubani who learned that her great grandfather was an slave trader named Oriaku Ogogo Nwaubani who was an famous slave trader in Nigeria whom gain his family wealth by selling other Africans to the white supremist who were willing to pay. Adaobi father would brag to her and said. "He was a renowned trader" Her father said with pride. "He dealt in palm produce and human beings." when Oriaku died too celebrate his life at his funeral they buried six enslaved Africans alive with Oriaku Ogogo Nwaubani dead body to honor this horrible race trader's life. Adaobi one day ask her father. "Are you not ashamed of what he did?" and Adaobi father responded back irritated. "Why should I be? His business was legitimate at the time. He was respected by everyone around." "Not everyone could summon the courage to be a slave trader, you had to have some boldness in you." This African coon said to his daughter like being an race trader was the hardest but bravest thing a man can do to earn his family a wealthy life. Now you can see how these immigrants can come over here in the united states and throw foundational Black Americans under the bus in order to make an decent life for their selves without blinking a eye, Because they see us only as slaves, Akatas, cotton pickers, We are nothing but an means for them to freeload off of our hard work and labor just like their doing right now in America. Another example of immigrant's coons is presidential candidate Kamala Harris who is half Jamaican and half Indian but only recently called herself an black woman, whereas before she was always Indian or Asian. But I'm not calling this woman an coonet because of what nationality she calls herself, No she's an coonet because of what she did to the black Community when she was an prosecutor and her stance of preparations. When Kamala Harris was the district attorney for Oakland California she enforce an Truancy policy that imprisoned single struggling mothers who mostly was black because their kids miss 10% of school (remember if you are late a number of times it counts as being absent from school.) which force single mothers to lose their jobs to support their children, causing families to be separated by foster care system because their mothers are doing 30 to 60 days in jail, because an child could have been absent because of illness or because an child might get to school every day but might be late often because of the mother's job and even the case of some fast ass teenagers 16-17 years old cutting school without you knowing until you get that report card, now you're in jail while you preschooler is taking away. Now she wants to apologizes because she trying to be President of the United States of America. Also this woman had the Authority to past an bill to enforce an Law to Investigate police shootings But like an good coonet she opposed the bill. But once you look at Kamala family ties you wouldn't be surprise at how she treats black people. Kamala father admitted that his grandmother Ne'e Christiana Brown aka Miss Chrishy Brown was an slave owners in Jamaica at the Hamilton Brown plantation. No wonder this woman said on television "I'm not doing anything that's just for Black people." when asked about reparations for F.B.A people. Speaking of immigrants and reparations the woman who made this H.R.40 Bill is an first generation American name Sheila Jackson Lee who parents immigrated in Queens New York from Jamaica. Besides this nothing bill I don't have much to say against Sheila accept that a person who truly haven't experience what

Foundational Black Americans had to endure for centuries and centuries of hell that carried on too the next generation, And every generation after wards, No, Hell no! No one should even have a say in nothing about reparations for F.B.A. Accept for fellow F.B.A. That like if I immigrated to Jamaica with my family and my grandchildren grow up to be politicians and have a legal say if Jamaicans can or can't have reparations from Spain & Britain for years of colonization that they did to the Jamaicans. We'll be lucky if they just deport us out of their country but all these immigrants get a say in what we should get or not. Get the hell out of here! Now finally the biggest con job done to us by an immigrant, an Immigrant who till this very day is looked at as the first African-American president of the united states of America. Yeah that's right I said it, I'm talking about former president Obama! Believe it or not this man wasn't even the first so called black president of the united states, Abraham Lincoln was. (Both was mulatto's by the way.) Abraham Lincoln mother Nancy, was having an affair with a black enslaved man who name believed was Iemis, on the plantation. Abraham himself described himself as "black and dark." when he ran for president. The newspaper called him "Negro" and made illustrations of him as an monkey. This is the why Abraham Lincoln is on the brown coin facing opposite of the rest of the presidents of the united states. This is to sham him and to show he's not like the rest of them (white people). Sadly former president Obama never gave an damn about black people period, Especially when this man can sign the Blue Alert law that helps enforce law enforcement because two police officers were killed in New York City because of the police murder of Freddie Gray in Baltimore. "They were serving their community with great honor and dedication and courage, And all of New York grieved and all of the nation grieved." This sellout that was suppose to be our first black president said for all the world to hear. I was living in new York city at that time and Obama is an damn liar, No foundational

Black American who wasn't involve with those cops didn't grieve for them. some of us actually said we wish the cops that got killed should of been white. We grieved for Eric Gardner, We grieved for Trayvon Martin, Sandra Bland, Micah Johnson and many more who lives who were taking during the Obama 8 years of presidency. This imposter continues to speak by saying. "It's important for us not only to honor their memory, it's also important for us to make sure that we do everything we can to help ensure the safety of our police officers when they're in the line of duty." How about you sign a form of protection for black Americans who are slaughter in the streets by these very same police officers who you endure so dearly Mr.Obama! Instead of calling black people who grew tired of the content oppression. "Criminals and Thugs who tore up the place." about black kids who riot because of the murder of Freddie Gray. But have never called out the officers that terrorizes us in the streets. No because he's not one of us but he was an great imposter, Had me fool with those speeches and F. B.A. Swag he had, yeah I learn real quick, that shit won't never happened again. Thank you Mr.Obama you help open up my eyes that all skin folks aren't kin folks. But to make things worst he sabotage his own people in Africa when he ordered the assassination of General Muammar Gaddfis. Don't believe the lies Muammar Gaddfis wasn't murdered because of humanitarian reasons but because he had an plan for a new African union base on African economics called the Gold Dinar. This currencies will be center on African gold instead of paper money currencies that the west and Europe uses. As you can see there is no place on the planted that have more gold and diamonds then the continent of Africa. Within ten years Africa will be the new super power and without white supremacy control over the world finances, white supremacy will be cripple beyond repair. No way American and the rest of the world leaders could allow such a thing, so do what you always do to stop an movement kill the head. And so it was done under the orders of an fellow black man name Obama. But betraying each other is nothing new. They can't even live among each other without enslaving and slaughtering each other for stupid reasons. They have a word for it called Xenophobia. Like in 1994 when the Hutu tribe slaughter over an million Tutsi people within months, or how even now as I write this in South Africa people are being killed because they originated from a different part of the land in Africa but yet the white man who stole your land and murdered and enslaved your people still living there in your land with all your riches as you all struggle for scraps. So after you finish killing the people that look like you because you all hate yourselves, Go and do that same thing to white man in your land... No? Yeah I know you can't. You couldn't dare do that to your lords and masters.

Chapter Nine

BECOME BLACK REVOLUTIONARIES

War is up on us, All of us weather we like it or not. The united states of American has set modern day **Jim crow** laws on us again. There isn't a place in America an black person could go without the slave patrol being called on them, simply just for being black. It doesn't matter if you're in the wrong or right, you will be treated as a criminal no matter what. The very fact that you have to discuss to your children how to conduct themselves self around police offers/ slave patrol, that is if you are a woke parent you would. Shows that you are in a state of war. We are not truly free, Our so called freedom is privilege until white supremacy decides to take your privileges away. Turning you in to a slave or taking your life when they feel the need to. Understand we do not have **rights only the illusion of them.** Rights are for white people while black people have privileges. This is why a person Sandra Bland could have a gun pulled out on her by an state trooper name Brian Encinia and forced out her car for not putting out a cigarette. She was roughly arrested as usual for black people. Then she was lynched in a cell with a garbage bag that was ruled a suicide. No justice was found. This woman was an revolutionary because she was an activist for black rights, this is what I believe was the real reason she was assassinated in jail. Melissa Mckinnies who help organize the protest against the police/ slave patrol murder of 18 year old Michael Brown Jr who was unarmed when shot and murdered by police offer Darren Wilson. Because of this woman's years of fighting for the liberation of black people rights to live, The white supremist killed her 24 year old son Danye Jones by **lynching** him in his mother's own back yard on a tree. Of course, the authority ruled it a suicide. Melissa knows what it truly was that's why she posted the murder of her own son on Facebook and said they killed her baby to pay her back, For all her years of protesting for the mistreatment of black lives. Another black protester in Ferguson Missouri was assassinated. His name was De Andre Joshua. Joshua was shot point blink in the head, One time execution style. Then was burned inside his vehicle to hide any evidence. During the same year Darren Seals 29 years old Ferguson activist who was shot dead and burned inside his vehicle as well. Shawn Gray 23 years of age was reported missing for six days after visiting his family on Thanksgiving, Before his lifeless body was found in River Des Peres. It was ruled an accident drowning. Of course his family didn't fall for the bull and believes he was murdered by the white supremist. Edward Crawford 27 years of age when he was shot dead another Ferguson activist. His death was ruled a suicide. The authorities claim that none of the Ferguson's assassinations were connected. Of course they were, they all are connected. If you are in these streets really trying to give black people the rights to their lives, Trying to stop the senseless murders and imprisonment of our people, you are the biggest threat to very foundation of America and you have to be dealt with. If the white supremacy can't get you to back off, sell out or pin charges on you, then they will try to kill you. Just like they did our brothers and sisters during the civil rights movement Martin Luther King Jr, Malcom X, Fred Hampton, Medgar Evers and many more of our falling revolutionaries throughout time. Minnesota an under rated racist state. Five Black Lives Matters protesters was shot by a white supremist name Allen Scarsella because they were protesting the death of

Jamar Clark who was assassinated by the slave patrol while he was on his back on the ground. By the grace of god the black lives matter activist wasn't killed by their gunshot wounds. Allen Scarsella was sentenced to 15 years in jail. Sometimes we are giving token justice here and there to control the uprising of the black people by giving us the illusion of justice. But we know that we won't never truly get true justice from this government, Not the way it is now. Understand that I'm not saying that everything is lost and that every black person who is woke to pick up arms and shot down the slave patrol and the white supremacy system that is the government. No it's not time to do such a thing yet, Because we will surly lose because there isn't enough of us that is woke to know how deep white supremacy is oppressing us, If they believe their oppress at all. We don't have no tactics or enough unity to pull off and sustain Guerrilla Warfare. One of my revolutionary's and falling Hero's was a man named Micah Xavier Johnson who killed five police offers/ slave patrollers while wounding nine more before they use one of their robots stripped with a bomb to kill him in a standoff. This was one man who stood up to our oppressors and took the fight to them because of the countless murders he saw his people endured. I respected what he did and understood it. Someone with Micah talents and knowledge of War fare would have been better used to teach his black people self defense tactics. His talent and skills went to waste on a suicide mission. Micah knew he wouldn't come back alive from. Micah died a warrior's death, May his soul rest in power. We in the black community must be smart on how we operate, we must educate each other how to survive and conquer the methods of white supremacy with out selling ourselves out becoming coons and coonets. Rakem Balogun was the first black man label as an **Black Identity Extremists.** Because of his out spoken views of police brutality and his community programs called Guerrilla mainframe that helps the black community with food while teaching them unarmed hand to hand combat and armed combat for self defense, Rakem group also use their 2nd amendment to bare arms to patrol their neiborhoods just like the black panthers did. The FBI surrounded this man house and arrested him and threw in jail for 6 months without a real lawyer and no bond understand the illegal act of Black Identity Extremists. Which is a modern day **COINTELPRO**. The FBI and CIA used during the civil rights movement to destroy the Black Panther Party of Self defense. Black civil rights leaders challenge the FBI and question them why are they targeting black people for basically being pro-black and nonviolent where as you have organization like Neo Nazis and Ku KLUX Klan who have been documented of murdering black people and those few white people who stood against the injustice of black people. Why there wasn't an White Identity Extremists. The FBI had no answers. We are hip to your game plans white supremist you won't destroy us using the same old tactics. like I said before we are survivors, we will learn to adapt to your evil tactics. You will not stop us from fighting for our liberation, you will not stop us with your slave patrol officers, you will not stop us with your coons and coonets, you will not stop us with your weapons of mass destruction. I made this book because I believe in black revolution. I have love ones very close to me who didn't want me protest, to make notice, let someone else fight the good fight, someone who don't have nothing to lose. Truth to be told I'm not no big name, I don't have followers or a YouTube channel or a part of an organization like Black Panthers Party. I'll be lucky if a hundred black people get to read this book. But I'm a man, A proud black man and I'm not going to sit by and not do anything to help the movement. I'll will play my part no matter how small it may be. I know when I look at my children and when they see me they know their father tried to do something against white supremacy to make their lives safer and closer to truly being free in this land, that our people build that's called the United States of America. These are but an few things we must get across this corrupt system if we are to be truly free without shedding blood. First understand we do not have no friends in this world. Most white people are our enemies because they are white supremist or white supremist sympathizers. Most Native Americans are your enemies, Especially the Cherokee Indians, All of you who brag that you have Indian in your or Cherokee in your blood, that's because your ancestors were their slaves and great great grandmothers was rape, for you to get that ' so called good hair' you keep bragging about. Arabs/ middle eastern people are not your friends, they were enslaving us before the white man and still are enslaving Africans till this very day and time. Asian people are one of the biggest white supremist people out there. Forget how they treat us in their stores in the U.S.A, If you go to Korea, japan, china you still will run in to black face and Jim crow dolls display in the open in their countries. And finally the Latin's, Hispanics they're not your friends ether, those black Hispanics that consider themselves black or Afro-Latin's this doesn't apply to you but too those who disown their black heritage especially the Hispanics who hang around you and call you my Nigga, then turn around and call you a Nigger or Moana. Use you as a shield to fight for their rights to come this country and once they're here, Turn on you and join groups like the Neo Nazi, Ku Klux Klan or the police and beat your ass with their new white privileges. You have no friends so stop trying to help other people in their problems, Let them handle their own shit cause no one is helping us when we need it. Liberal or conservative which should we vote for? My opinion don't vote nether until they have a black agenda. Not for color people or minority because those labels include all types of nationality's and groups. No, No we need a policy for black people only, if you don't have representatives that will speak up for us like London Lamar did or Marianne Williamson on reparations and how Eritha Akile

Cainion a young black sista who is standing up for our people against gentrification in St. Pete Florida. Then we don't vote at all until our reparations are paid for. Use that money to build black economics and pay for our own politicians who will grant laws that will empower black people in this country. 1. Any police offer kills an unarmed black man or woman will be automatic charge with manslaughter and the charge can only go up. 2. black people are in title to have what we earned which is cash reparations for slavery, black Codes, Jim Crow, Cointelpro, Black Identity Extremists and everything else this country has done to us. We will be giving our own land and treated as an sovereignty state. 3. Change the 13th amendment, erase the nor or accept part of that bill, you are free period there will be no slavery in the united states of America period. Foundational black Americans will boycott this whole entire system until we are paid the dept we are owned for building this country. That's my black agenda give us what you own us! Tell the democrats that when you want to vote for them in office. Put one of those on your policy. Like I said before we all should have a part to play in freeing our people. I'm Tyrik Cogdell, I'm a black man that writes books in order too help wake up our people from the imprisonment of white supremacy and the founder of the Black Power Of Self Defense in order to teach our men, women and children how to defend their selves and their love ones from racist attacks, Sex and harvest tracking against our people. That's what I'm doing for the black cause, So what are you going to do? Black power to all my people!

Chapter Ten

MIND SET FOR REVOLUTION

As a black person in America you must know you are an prisoner of war, Especially if you are FBA (foundational black Americans) You have to understand that this entire system of Government is made to exploit us and enslave us, But in order to achieve this without physical push back. White supremacy wants us to believe we are free, But it's all illusions. We are not free, we are prisoners in our own land and must of us don't know it or refuse to acknowledge it. We are being killed in these streets by modern day slave patrol officers with impunity, while being imprisoned in slavery with long jail sentences for minor crimes or crimes we've haven't committed at all to enrich white supremacy through slave labor just like our ancestors in chattel slavery. Our women and children are being kidnap and force to be sex slaves, Our people are being murdered for our organs to sale on the black market on in the name of white supremacy. If you continues to walk around believing in an post-racial America as an black person, you will not survive unless you convert and become an full fledged traitor-coon against the black community. We must acknowledge that we don't have no allies in this fight against white supremacy, Even most of our own brothers and sisters across the globe is in support of white supremacy. This is something that we must accept if we are to survive and conquer white supremacy and their non-white allies. We are at war and you must act accordingly if we are to win this war my brothers and sisters. Revolution, Liberation won't happened on its own, Every one who is about black liberation have to be involve, you can't just wait around for someone else to save you, you have to be willing to fight for yourself. In the words of Kendrick Lamar: "who needs a hero? You need a hero, look in the mirror, there go your hero." you have to be able to fight for yourself in order to liberate yourself, Only cowards are willing slaves and coons. In order to be a black revolutionary, you have to be willing to stand up for what you believe in, Rather if that's online or in person. Handing out flyers, Talking in council halls, Black media outlets, Writing books, Educating our people on their greatness and how to grow, Protesting or boycotting for black liberation. We are at war my people and once you accept this, That is the very first step in your survival against white supremacy. Now that you understand who your enemies are and understand our living situation under the enemy, you must learn how to conduct yourselves around the enemy if we are to survive. Everyday you step outside your door you should be mentally ready to deal with an white supremist regardless if it's an civilian or law enforcement. With that as an mind set you won't be surprise when an situation occurs with these racist bastards. Once your mind is ready to accept that we as black people have no allies and that we are prisoners of war who must liberate ourselves and love ones by any means necessary, then you are truly ready to survive and conquer what the white supremist brings your way. Have the mindset of black Revolutionaries my people.

Chapter Eleven

THE METAL AND PHYSICAL TOOLS OF WAR AGAINST THE OPPRESSORS

As a black person in American you must be able to defend yourself and your love ones from harm. There are different routes of doing this depending on the situation, situations that I will cover in this chapter, but first we will start with the most basic human defense which is hand to hand combat. As a black man, Husband and father of three children I believe that every black person should know how to handle themselves physically with and without weapons. Remember we are prisoners of war, and if you are in an prison you best to know how to defend yourself and how to move around your enemies. I teach my people how to defend their selves and their love ones in an studio that I call Black Power of self-defense. This is highly important for our people more then it ever was because none of us, None of us are safe now. Our children are being kidnapped and smuggle for sex trafficking and to have their organ harvest on the black market and the white elite. The very same thing is happening to our women, Especially for their ovaries because the white woman low birth rates and bodies are not well enough to bare children so they are using our black women and children as spare parts. Our men are being killed for harvest organs as well but not in an large clip as our little girls and women because the white supremist loves soft targets. Don't be fooled the white supremist isn't the only ones doing the abducting our sellouts and Latin people are doing a lot of the heavy weight lifting in our community's, you must look out for them as well. Don't expect the cops to crack down on this because the government are the ones allowing this to happened in the first place, just like the police murder us in these streets with impunity along with their white supremist civilians who get away with murdering us like that bastard George Zimmerman. So my black people first take an hand to hand combat course. Nothing fancy learn something simple but very efficient, nothing that take years to learn because to be able to pull off those techniques in high stress situations it will take years in order to perform in an real life self-defense situation and you still might lock up with pressure. Learn an jab, straight punch, an hook, elbow, knee, kick in the groin, leg sweep and how to stomp along with learning how to stop an take down attempt is how you need to know to defend your self from any attacker if you don't have any weapons on you. It will only take a matter of weeks to learn the techniques and months to master them all. That is the true key of unarmed hand to hand self-defense. Next you must learn how to use weapons and I'm talking about modern self-defense weapons not the exotic kung fu stuff you see in the movies. Of course, learning how to use an gun and having one is the best weapon you could use for self-defense but unfortunately every state won't allow you to carry guns like New York city, just having an license to have an gun in your home is hell to get. You will need to learn how to use smaller, lethal and non-lethal weapons to protect yourself and your love ones. You should always Carrie an knife an small tactical one at that, too make it hard for your attacker to see and defend themselves from it. Bear mace or strong mace with dye that can blind your attacker, some states this kind of mace is illegal like New York city once again but an charge is better being dead or an sex slave which is the same thing to me. Tasers are very good, an taster gun which also is illegal in NYC (pretty much everything you could use to fend someone off is off limits in this damn city.) or taser rod and brass knuckles are very handy tools of defense. Teach yourself, Teach your children these things because their and your lives depends on it, such is the way of war. And we are the targets that everyone has declare war on and now is our time too do the ass kicking and show these invaders that black people will not be wiped out because we are going to be the ones who cleanse out white supremacy and all their supporters. Lastly and this is especially for the black men out here. Keep your self in good shape physically, there are too many small brothers out here that can't fight worth a damn these days, that's one among many reasons these civilian white supremist feel like they can approach you and call you all types of niggers in your face. Walking around with pants hanging down to your knees aren't going to help you kick some white supremist ass that decides to test you one day. You as black men are the warriors of the black race, you are the protectors so it's time to get on your stuff and start acting like it. All soldiers of war are fit soldiers that can spring in to action with in an blink of an eye. Us as black men are the soldiers on the front line because an people without their men to lead and protect are doom as the war is over before it could even begin. Once you have the mindset that we as black people are in war and you are physically really defending yourselves and loved ones in this world, you must be able to defend yourselves from the corrupt laws of this white supremacy government. One of the ways is to weaponize your camera phones. Every encounter that you have with an slave patrol officer or you see another black person having an encounter with them stop and start recording. Because if it's your word against theirs, you will lose every time. If you are being harassed by these terrorist start recording imminently, Quickly state that your rights is being violated and how, then apply to the slave patrol officers demands without another saying another word so they can't hit you up with resisting arrest charges. Remember that we are prisoners of war so how we move and conduct ourselves around these racist bastards is an matter of life and death to us. Now that your privilege rights are being violated you can sue the department of injustice and maybe, maybe but not likely could get the slave patrol officer fired as well. I understand that you're thinking why do I have to take this kind of mistreatment we have rights, but like I was saying before we really don't have rights in this country, we have the illusion of having rights, The bill of rights wasn't written for us, An bill in it's very own 13th amendment states that slavery is very much still legal in this so called land of the free. (Free for the white man) like I said you have to know how to move around your enemies if you want to survive in this world without selling out your soul and your people. If you see a fellow black brother or sister be harassed by the slave patrol stop whatever you're doing and start recording, shout out the officers are doing wrong and don't go nowhere. If you feel that they are taking their actions to far step forward as you record what terrorism these racist slave patrol officers are doing to our people while shouting out "you killing him or her! You murdering him or her!" this will cause an delay in the slave patrol assault on the black person they were abusing and bring their attention towards you, telling you to step back. Just with that interruption alone you must likely saved an brother and sister from being murdered in the street. It's not stopping police brutality but it can save an fellow brother and sister to survive another day. Now the most dangerous being pulled over while being black. Every time you are pulled over there is an 50% chance you could be the next unarmed black person to be murdered in their own car. I personally never bother to learn how to drive because of this, as an child I would prefer to them as death mobiles because all the time I looked an black man was being harassed or killed by some racist slave patrol officer, plus I didn't like highways. It is known for these slave patrol officers to plant drugs in your car in order to arrest you to force you to become not only an mental slave and an prisoner of war but an legal physical slave as well on their modern day plantations called the prison complex. If you are lucky you would only be harassed and have your ID ran through the system for no reason and giving an personal lecture as if you were some sort of child before being sent on your way. The unlucky black people or the ones who are shoot dead in the seats of their cars by trigger happy slave patrol officers. There are a few ways to avoid being the next dead black person on FOX NEWS and CNN. Number one have cameras installed in your car. Have it in plan sight in front and the rear of your car. Tell the slave patrol officer that everything is being recorded as soon as you think the slave patrol is enforcing his racism injustice up on you. Also have cameras installed in hidden areas like under your seat or the arm between the seats of the car, this can protect you when one of these slave patrol officers tries to plant drugs or weapons in your vehicle in order to frame you. Second once you see that you are being pulled over by the slave patrol, have your ID, registration and anything else you would need on the dash board along with both of your hands place flat on the dash board as well. Never, Never reach for anything, even if the cop gives you permission to do so, don't do it! Tell them where the object is and give them permission to get it themselves while keeping extremely still and calm, A skill I learned in an very young age, that saved my life against this racist slave patrol officers on more then one situation. Next and the last thing you need to know to survive these type of encounters with these bastards is to keep your emotions in check and be very calm. They hate that shit because they like to bate you in to reacting to them. This is where the mind set of being an prisoner of war comes through because you understand you are not an American civilian with rights by an prisoner of war with privileges until you can over throw this corrupt government of white supremacy and recapture your land that our ancestors build while we continues to keep this country running off our blood and sweat till this very day. When the slave patrol officer asks you for your information without good reason, give it to him or her without argument. Then ask why are they pulling you over and state what they doing is violating your rights as an American civilian. (I'm not conducting myself, we are prisoners of war but the white suprema-cist wants to give you the illusion that you are free so you have to know how to play the game. This is one of the ways when I say learn how to move around your enemies.) once you state this on camera, regardless of what he or she say's do not argue and do what they ask and go by your way and sue, securing yourself and your family an nice money bag for your troubles. These are your weapons in order to survive this world of white supremacy. One of the very first rules I learned as an young black boy was too never trust the police. The police, the feds and all other type of law enforcement in this corrupt government that is called the United States of America is, and always will be our greatest enemies as black people. The soon-er you learn this, the better your chances of surviving this white supremacy system of black oppression. As an black person you should never, Ever call 9-1-1. Unless you or some one you know is sick to the point where you or your people are seriously hurt or straight dying you don't never! Ever call the police/ slave patrol for any kind of help. The slave patrol was the original police officer of this country. Their duties were never to protect us but to return us to our slave masters and murder us if we get out of hand, No differ-ent from 1703 then it is today in 2021. They had an oath to swear themselves in as slave patrollers. "I (patroller's name) do swear, that I will as searcher for guns, swords and other weapons among the slaves in my district faithfully and as privately as I can, discharge the trust reposed in me as the law districts, to the best of my power. So help me god." the slave patrol oath of North Carolina in 1828. Don't sound no different then what the police do to us today. Calling these racist bastards for any reason right or wrong can lead to your death or if you're lucky wrongful arrest. Remember how an black man name Bryant Heyward how was burglarize and he called 9-1-1 and they shot this man in his neck in his own home, Now he's paralyzed from his neck down for the rest of his life. Then there was a black young woman by the name of Dyma Loving who called 9-1-1 because an white pulled out an shotgun on Loving and her friend as they walked by his house yelling out how he's going to blow their brains out. When the slave patrol arrived they didn't approach the racist gun owner who threaten this young black woman's life, No instead they interrogated this woman until she was almost in tears and when she had enough and called them on their bullshit the slave patrol officers abuse this woman by slamming her to the ground and arresting her. What about Travis Jordan an young black man who was suffering from depressions and had suicidal thoughts so his girlfriend called 9-1-1 and explained to them to check on him and that he planned on killing himself. The slave patrol decides to break in to Travis apartment finding a knife in his hand because he's doesn't know who the hell is breaking in to his house, decides to shoot and murder Mr.Jordan instead saving him from killing him-self. Doing the complete opposite what the girlfriend sent them out there to do. The old isn't spared in these wellness 9-1-1 calls ether, Not if they are black their not. Kenneth Chamberlain senior an 68 year old black veteran and James Allen an 74 year old military vet-eran as well, both black, both serve their country's and survived wars only for the both of them to have their houses broke in to and executed by slave patrol officers paid by the same government that they once served. This is the true purpose of the slave parolee's. Too harassed, arrest and bring you down in to physical slavery or too murder you with impunity. This is our reality and we must do everything possible to stop the oppression of our people. I have an long history of martial arts experience along with defending myself successfully against knife attacks and surviving white supremacist with guns in my life time. I'm sharing some self defense illustrations of ways to defend yourself from attacks so, you can make home back to your family. Some of the demonstrations here will seem extreme, because these techniques can very well cause death to-wards your attackers. But some laws these methods are beyond simple self-defense so only use these techniques if you feel your life depends on it. Better to be hit with an charge and fight for your freedom then being dead by some race soldier or their non-white bootlicks or harvest for your organs and being sex traffic where you being raped everyday can be worst then death in my opinion. Having an gun is the best defense but of course a lot of us don't have one or not allow to Carrie a fire arm like new York city. These techniques are base off of weapons that can easily be carried in your pockets and won't leave a trace back too you like gun shells.

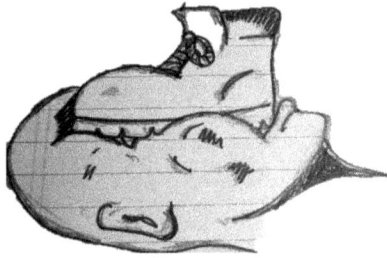

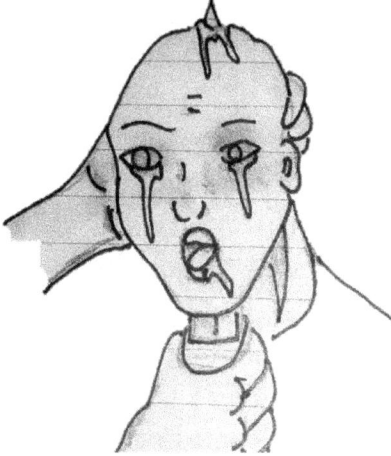

The first illustration is how to defend yourself from your oppressor and his bootlicks with Hand to hand combat using brass knuckles. Kick the oppressor in the groin follow up with A strong straight punch then leg sweep the oppressor to the ground, following up with multiple Strikes towards the face, finishing them off with a stomp. The second illustration is you backing your oppressor off you With a forearm to the chin or upper chest while stabbing your Attacker multiple times in the chest, stomach or lower area And finishing your oppressor with grabbing the back of your oppressor's Head and stabbing your knife though their head or neck. The last defense is when an oppressor is trying to harm you take Out a small hair spray and spray it lighting the fumes on fire Burning the oppressor in their face or chest where ever you can get them at. Remember these illustrations will work but be warn in the eyes of the White supremacy law these self defense techniques won't go in your Favor in the court of law. But I am showing you how to survive keeping Yourself and your love ones alive. So make sure your live is on the line When applying these techniques. Black first my peoples.

Chapter Twelve

ROHOWA

Rohowa means the Racial Holy War to white supremist. And I agree this is an racial holy war that goes back to biblical times. When it comes to race I don't like getting in to religion to much because everyone is not a believer but to break down Rohowa which is a holy war up on us stated by the white supremist themselves I have no choice but to get biblical. First to understand their blind pure hatred of us you must understand where they came from. Those who believe in god would simply just call them devils but it's a lot deeper than just calling someone devils because of their evil ways. But before I break down where and what the white man is I have to explain what and who we are in the eyes of the lord and savior. When God made man in his own image he made Adam from dirt, what color is dirt? Dirt is black, Dirt is brown but dirt is never white. This is your first clue in the bible that black people are the original people of this world. The second is the biggest revelation and it comes from the book of Enoch, which use to be cannon and the most popular book in the old testament. Noah's birth is describe in this scripture. "After a time, My son Mathusala took a wife for his son Lamech. She became pregnant by him, And brought forth a child, The flesh of which was as white of snow, and red as a rose, the hair of whose head was white like wool, and long; and eyes were beautiful. When he opened them, He illuminated all the house, like the sun; The whole house abounded with light. And when he was taken to the midwife, opening also his mouth, He spoke to the lord of righteousness. Then Lamech his father was afraid of him; and flying away came his father Mathusala, and said, I have begotten a son, Unlike to other children. He is not human; but resembling the offspring of the angels of heaven, is of a different nature from ours, being altogether unlike us." Book of Enoch 105;1-3 Did you catch all of that? They said Noah's was white as snow, and his hair was white and like wool. This show's that Noah was an albino because of his skin color was white as snow plus his hair was white. And albino have what they call white blonde hair and the texture was of wool which the Caucasian man do not have unless one of their parents are indeed black. More to prove that the original people were black was how the grandfather and father of Noah was scare because they said he resemble the children of the angels of heaven. Which meant what? That the children of angels was white. But they wasn't albino white they were Caucasian white, the Nephilim the seed of the fallen angels who had children with our black women. Remember that they said the offspring of the angels were unlike us that they were of an different nature, telling you that everyone was the opposite of white. The Nephilim's were only good for destruction, they killed, murdered for fun and consumed everything and then they started to consume the flesh of man. Which were black people an tradition that continues throughout history and our present day. They were an abomination to our lord and savior so he flooded the earth killing most of the Nephilim but they all didn't die unfortunately. Because throughout the bible the original Hebrews had to fight the descendants of the Nephilim race which were the Anakims, philistines, the Greeks and the Romans throughout history. Knowing this now the bible looks like an old historic book of an race war between the black race and the white race. Remember the fear of an black messiah, by the head of the F.B.I J.Edgar Hoover who said their goals was to. "Prevent the rise of a messiah who could unify and electrify the militant black nationalist movement. Malcolm X might have been such a messiah. Martin Luther king, Stokely Carmichael, Elijah Muhammed all aspire to this position. King could be a very real contender for this position should he abandon his supposed obedience to white liberal doctrines." he said. Every prophet in the bible was a black revolutionary leader, Don't think that just because it's not on paper that King & Malcom X wasn't prophets because the white government of white supremacy sure in hell felt like they were. Even the image of one of our greatest revolutionary leaders the one that everyone call the true messiah was stolen from us, His name was Jesus Christ. That's right just like every other prophet in the bible was an black person and so was Jesus Christ. The imposter you see in the churches, movies, statues, candies and any other image around the world is an lie. That brown long hair pale face man is not Jesus Christ but a man named Cesare Borgia the son of the pope Alexander VI. Pope Alexander the VI wanted to immortalize his son image as god while fooling the world by making the new generation of white people believe they are an superior race while the black race feel like the inferior race. Unfortunately, this planed work because till this very day with all the proof of the world people will still believe Jesus and god is white. But for those of us that can see things for what there truly are I'll show you proof that the Jesus Christ was an black man. Jesus Christ description was revealed in the bible. "The hair of his head were white, like white wool. Like snow. His eyes were like a flame of fire, his feet were like burnished bronze, Refined in a furnace, and his voice was like the roar of many waters." Jesus had white hair made like wool with burnished bronze skin color which is an very, very dark brown color. Another example of Jesus being a black man was the true manor of his death. Jesus was murdered like any other black man in the hands of white supremacy, this is the proof. "The god of our fathers raised up Jesus whom ye slew and Hanged on a tree." did you get that? Jesus was hanged on a tree in other words Jesus was lynched just like we, as black people are lynch till this very day. Need further proof. "Now when they had fulfilled all that was written concerning him. They took him down from the tree and laid him in a tomb." Jesus followers had to take his body down from hanging from a tree. A damn tree. You see it now Jesus was an black revolutionary who walk among his people, Helping them and scolding the Coons of the black community who benefited with their positions of power allowed by the white man and had the Judas among his mist who sold him out, just like many other great black prophets that was sold out by our own people. The fear of the black messiah is real, Then and now for the white supremist. Did you know that white supremist groups are connected with Satanism, they are many satanic neo-Nazi groups that support each other ideology like the Order of nine angels, The ordo sinistra Vivendi, joy of Satan and the Esoteric Hitlerism and many, many more white supremist groups. One of the most common sign of these unholy groups are the okay sign. That's what we called it when I was growing up, when your index finger and your thumb connects together to make a circle while the remaining three fingers stay up slightly bend forward. This hand sign represents the mark of the beast, Six hundred and sixty six but this very same sign is also use as the letter 'W' which stands for white power. You'll see it all over television, Especially by the president of the united states of America and other government officials. Regardless if you believe all the biblical talk, Believe this that the white supremist who ready themselves for Rohowa believes it, And that's enough reason for them to shoot you down like an infested horde of rats in the streets and lynch you in the back yard of your homes while raping and murdering your wife and children. The holy war is here, The racial war is here if you accept it or not. God has been doing his part by declining their birth rates but now it's time for us to ready our minds and bodies for war because they won't stop, The killings will continues and you as black people are going to have to make a choice. Like the great Malcolm x said "I'm telling you, you don't know what a revolution is. Cause when you find out what it is, you'll get back in the alley; you'll get out the way. The Russian Revolution-what was it base on? Land. The land-less against the landlord. How did they bring it about? Bloodshed. You haven't got a revolution that doesn't involve bloodshed. And you're afraid to bleed. I said you're afraid to bleed." so my black people stop being afraid to bleed because the white man is making us bleed anyway, And if I'm going to bleed, I'm sure in hell is going to make them bleed too! **wake up black people or die**!

**Special thanks to those that supported me,
And those who were scare for my safety.**

Thank you to my beautiful wife Morningstar thank you to my lovely three children Gabriella, Logan and Brandon. Thank you to the woman who gave me life my mother Regina and her family. To my dad I thank you too Irving. I also thank my one and only uncle Earl. I also thank my late grandparents Mattie and Charles for the love they showed me growing up. I thank my late grandparents Wilbert and Ruth for raising me to be the man that I am today. Thank you and thank you to the rest of my family that supported me and looked out for me. Black power to all my people!

www.ingramcontent.com/pod-product-compliance
Lightning Source LLC
Chambersburg PA
CBHW060555100426
42742CB00013B/2567